D1826027

Back cover top: The Ar 234 V2 experimental aircraft, photographed just after leaving the runway for its first flight at Alt-Lönnewitz in Lower Saxony with the aid of two 500kg thrust Walter RI 202 rocket-assisted take-off units, 13 September 1943. This second prototype (DP+AW, *Werk Nr.* 130002) was destroyed on 10 October 1943 when one engine caught fire. The pilot, *Flugkapitän* Selle, on his sixth flight in the V2, was killed.

Back cover bottom: The first comparative testing between the He 280 V7 and V8 was planned for October 1944, but because it proved impossible to equip the latter with a 'vee' tail until the end of 1944 flying was temporarily discontinued. The ultimate fates of these 'high-speed gliders' is unknown, but they were probably scrapped during the summer of 1945. The photograph shows the seventh He 280 with its special calibration equipment, awaiting action at a snowy Ainring (Bavaria) airfield.

1. On 7 January 1945 *KG 51* staff flight had four Me 262 bombers, 30 others were operated by *I Gruppe*, *II Gruppe* owned ten and a further nine were supposedly on their way to the *Geschwader*. By mid-January about 49 Me 262 'Blitzbombers' were actually on strength, and some jets were flown to Rhein-Main airfield to begin operations against advancing Allied ground forces near Strasbourg, which was liberated by French troops on 18 January. During February *I* and *II Gruppe* of *KG 51* operated against enemy concentrations in Kleve and the Rhineland.

WARBIRDS ILLUSTRATED No 52

German JETS
of World War Two

MANFRED GRIEHL

ARMS & ARMOUR PRESS

London   New York   Sydney

Introduction

First published in Great Britain in 1988 by Arms & Armour Press Ltd., Artillery House, Artillery Row, London SW1P 1RT.

Distributed in the USA by Sterling Publishing Co. Inc., 2 Park Avenue, New York, NY 10016.

Distributed in Australia by Capricorn Link (Australia) Pty. Ltd., P.O. Box 665, Lane Cove, New South Wales 2066.

British Library Cataloguing in Publication data:
Griehl, Manfred.
German jets of World War Two.
1. Germany, Luftwaffe. Military aeroplanes: 1939–1945
I. Title II. Series
623.74′6′0903

ISBN 0-85368-884-2

Edited and designed by Roger Chesneau.
Printed and bound in Great Britain by
The Bath Press.

◀2
2. *Leutnant* Franz Schall, the commander of *10/JG 7 'Nowotny'*, whose Me 262A-la was shot down by American fighters on 4 April 1945. He survived this crash but a was killed few days later when his Me 262 rolled into a crater and exploded. He had achieved twenty victories and was the third highest-scoring jet fighter pilot in the *Luftwaffe* after *1/Lt.* Kurt Welter of *11/NJG 11* (formerly *Kommando 'Welter'*) with 28 'kills' and *2/Lt.* Rudolf Rademacher of *11/JG 7* with 25. Schall's first victory in the Me 262 came on 8 November 1944, the day *Major* Nowotny was killed in action.

This *Warbirds Illustrated* volume contains many new photographs of the German jet-powered aircraft which, within a few short years, changed the face of aviation. The book does not deal solely with the famous Me 262 (although more than 1,500 examples were built, under incredible conditions), since as well as this and the new '*Volksjäger*' designs a lot of other interesting fighter projects were under development during the final six months of the Second World War: Focke-Wulf, Gotha, Heinkel, Henschel, Horten, Junkers and some smaller concerns all embarked on the project definition of high-speed interceptors to stop the Allied bomber fleets over the Reich, while advanced Messerschmitt designs, for example the P.1101 and 1112, were beginning to open the door for the supersonic fighter aircraft. Clearly, the days of the piston-engined fighter were numbered, despite powerful German types like Kurt Tank's Ta 152 and the many fast, long-range Allied fighter aircraft such as the P-51 Mustang.

Together with the Me 262 '*Blitzbomber*', the Arado 234 and Junkers 287 appeared to herald new ways of promoting an offensive air war. The Ar 234 entered service in October 1944 and went into action at the end of December that year as the first true jet bomber, but, hampered by its troublesome engines and the chaotic fuel situation in Germany in 1944–45, it was unable to halt the Allied advance. After some desperate attacks, which succeeded in hindering the Rhine crossing, the operational career of the 234 was brought to a close in March 1945. For its part, the Ju 287 proved to be nothing more than an interesting signpost along the road to the development of the modern bomber aircraft.

Thus although the new German jets flew numerous sorties, the cause was obviously lost by the time they had reached the squadrons, and the 'high-tech' aircraft were too few in number to exercise an influence on the course of the war. The new technology required refined materials and improved aerodynamic principles, which would take time to develop, and these factors, together with the innumerable small technical problems which arose, prevented the German aircraft industry from realizing its ambitious plans to create an entirely new generation of warplanes before the war ended: except for the Me 262 and the He 162, none of the fast turbine aircraft really got a chance.

I should like to express my sincere thanks to many good friends in Australia, Britain, Germany, Switzerland and the United States for their assistance in preparing this book. Special thanks go to Messrs. Creek, Dabrowski, Dierich, Dressel, Francella, Heck, Lutz Jr., Maesel, Martinez, Mohr, Muth, Nowarra, Pervesler, Radinger, Riedinger, Rohrbach, Schliepharke, Spencer, Selinger, Stapfer, Trenkle, Wegmann, Zucker and many others, and to the Forschungsgruppe, Luftfahrtgeshichte e.V., Heinkel GmbH, Dr. Hiller, Messrs Ebert and Roosenboom of MBB Bremen and Munich, and NASM. Without the help given by these individuals and organizations this volume would not have been possible.

Manfred Griehl

E 02347020 V6

3, 4. Two photographs of the Ar 234 V6 (GK + IW, *Werk Nr.* 130006), which flew for the first time on 8 April 1944; the aircraft is sitting on its undercarriage trolley, and a mobile external engine starter is evident in each view. The BMW 003 powerplant proved to be extremely troublesome. Both photographs were taken at the Arado works at Alt-Lönnewitz in mid-March 1944.

5. The sixth Ar 234 on its undercarriage trolley, showing the excellent forward visibility from the glazed cockpit. Note the trio of skids under the main fuselage and the engines nacelles. The skid landing system was chosen after several proposals shown on project drawings of the Ar E 370 jet bomber with two early Jumo TLs and the smaller BMW P 3302. The Ar 234 V6 logged only 3hrs 18mins of flying time before it crashed on 1 June 1944.

6. The eighth Ar 234 prototype (GK + IY, 130008) was powered by four BMW 003 turbojets in paired nacelles. First flown on 4 February 1944, it was severely damaged in a crash on 6 May 1944 after having been flown by Arado test pilot Janssen on about six occasions. The ultimate fate of the Ar 234 V8 is unknown.

7. The Ar 234 V9 was the most widely tested military prototype among the early jet-engined Arados. PH + SQ (130009) was tasked with carrying different payloads, e.g. three 500kg GP bombs or a heavy SC 1000 bomb under the centreline. The first flight took place on 12 March 1944, and in April the aircraft started bombing trials, carrying the SC 1000 and two additional Walter RI 202 rocket engines beneath each inner wing section. The aircraft was last heard of in December 1944, after successfully completing more than 120 test flights.

8. In mid-August 1944 the first Ar 234 trials were undertaken using two 300-litre auxiliary drop tanks, installed on the ninth prototype, which was flown by Frach and Eheim, two very experienced Arado pilots. The tanks were fitted under the Jumo 004 turbojets and were equivalent in size to those fitted as a centerline store on the Fw 190 and Bf 109. By the end of the war some Ar 234B-1s had seen action with this equipment.

▼8

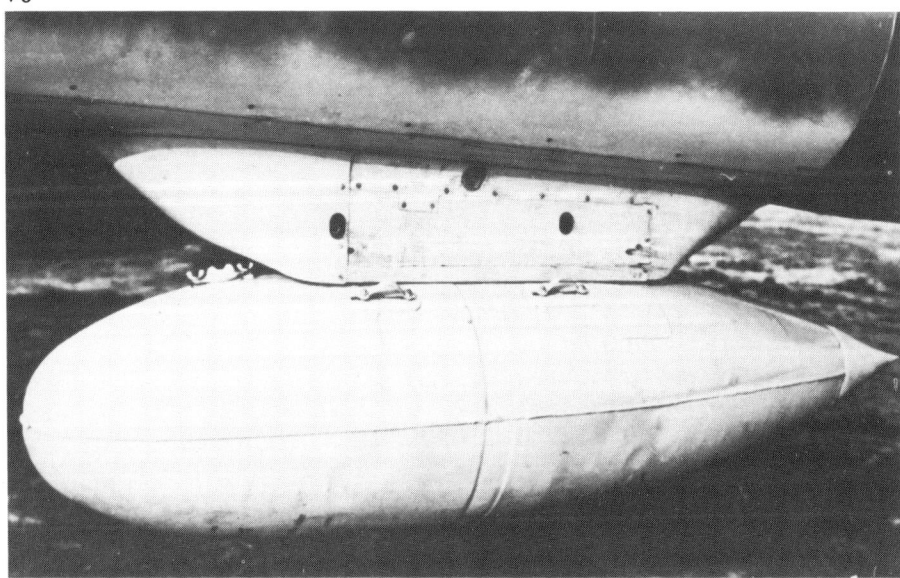

9. ▲

9. SC 500s were fitted to the Ar 234 V9 during trials with radio guidance systems involving the Arado test pilots Eheim and Kroeger. The latter reached an altitude of more than 12,000ft on 29 April 1944, the Ar 234 V9 then being brought into a glide and its parachute brake deployed. These early trials were interrupted when Allied bombers were reported over central Germany, and the next tests were curtailed because of severe problems with the aircraft's engines.

10. The Ar 234 V13, rolled out at Sommer in 1944, and flying for the first time on 6 September that year, was the third four-engined Arado prototype. Janssen was selected to pilot the aircraft on its maiden flight – a sortie which also proved to be its last. One of the BMW 003A-1 engines caught fire, and in the subsequent emergency landing the aircraft was badly damaged. The remains were transferred to the *Luftwaffe*'s Technical School at Jüterborg for training purposes.

10. ▼

▲11

11. Only two BMW 003 A-1s were fitted to the Ar 234 V17 (PI + SÝ, *Werk Nr.* 130027), which was first flown on 25 September 1944. The aircraft was based at Küpper and Sorau until 10 October, later moving to Oranienburg and Lärz airfields. On 22 March it reached an altitude of 31,500ft. The following April, the V17 was transferred to Lechfeld in Bavaria and subsequently to Neubiberg near Munich, where it was destroyed by German forces a short time before the arrival of Allied ground troops.

12. The Ar 234 V20 (PI + WY, *Werk Nr.* 130030) was first flown, by Janssen, on 5 November 1944 at Küpper aerodrome; six days later it ran into an Fw 190 on the ground and Janssen was injured. After testing the bomber at Küpper airfield, Eheim flew the V20 from Alt-Lönnewitz to Brandenburg-

Briest, but by the end of the war it had been withdrawn to Rostock-Warnemünde. The ultimate fate of this aircraft is unknown, but there is some evidence that it was destroyed during further trials in March 1945.

13, 14. Two views of the engine installation in the four-engined Ar 234 V19 (*Werk Nr.* 130029, PI + WX), one of four Arado jets still flying by the end of 1944. On 19 January 1945 the aircraft's starboard undercarriage collapsed, and it proved difficult to complete repairs because of the many air raids taking place and the shortage of spare parts. On 7 February 1945, however, the aircraft arrived at Brandenburg-Briest, where engine development trials continued until the end of March. On 4 April 1945 the V19 was damaged for a second time and never flew again.

▼12

13▲   14▼

▲15

15. The prototype for the Ar 234C series was the Ar 234 V21 (PI + WZ, *Werk Nr.* 130061), which started flight trials on 24 November 1944 and was still in use in March 1945. Production of the Ar 234C-3 began in February 1945 at Alt-Lönnewitz, and a second line, at Brandenburg, was planned to open later. There were firm orders for more than 1,500 Ar 234C-3 bombers and 330 C-4 reconnaissance aircraft, while a further 1,400 two-seat bombers and 290 night-fighters (Ar 234C-7) were projected. However, the C-1 and C-2 were abandoned in favour of the Ar 234B-1 and B-2.

16. Another view of the Ar 234 V21, the sole C-series prototype to be equipped with two MG 151/20 in the rear fuselage section (one of the rearward-facing gun troughs can be seen in this port-side view of the aircraft). Four further Ar 234s each with four BMW 003A-1s were built, designated Ar 234 V22 to V25. The V25 flew at Küpper for the first time and was brought to Briest on 2 February 1945; in April it was declared operational at Warnemünde and on 1 May flown by Eheim to Kaltenkirchen, where *I/JG 7* was standing by.

▼16

17. Ar 234C-3 250006 was one of the few four-engined Arado jet bombers ever to become operational. About a dozen were completed at Brandenburg-Neuendorf, whilst a further 8–10 awaited only their engines. Three C-3s had been transferred to *Ergänzungskampfgeschwader 1* at Alt-Lönnewitz by the end of March 1945. Very few Ar 234C-4s had been built and flown by the end of the war.
18. The aircraft of the commander of the famous *Kampfgeschwader 76* is here towed by a Kettenkrad, typical

ground-handling equipment for German jet units during the last months of the Second World War. The photograph of *Major* Bätcher's Ar 234B-2 (Fl + AD) was taken at Burg near Magdeburg in central Germany in 1945. Bätcher had carried out some glide-bombing and low-level attacks with SD 500 GP bombs against enemy tank concentrations near Kalkar and Kleve during February 1945, as well as flying some vital reconnaissance missions.

19. These two pilots, Götz and Heese, were members of the *Versuchsverband* of the *Oberkommando der Luftwaffe* (*VersVerb. OkL*). Both flew reconnaissance missions with the Ar 234B-1, (converted from standard Ar 234B-2 bombers to carry two cameras) from Rheine in November and December 1944 preparatory to the German Ardennes offensive. The aircraft of *Kommando 'Sperling'* (Sparrow), a part of the *Versuchsverband*, bore the official code 'T9'.

20. One of *Oberleutnant* Horst Götz's few Arado Ar 234B-1s preparing for flight, in late 1944. *Kommando 'Sperling'* was in due course incorporated into *1(F)/123* and withdrawn from Rheine (in western Germany) to Rheinsehlen on 23 March. On 6 April the last surviving jet reconnaissance aircraft landed at Blankensee near Lübeck on the Reichsautobahn, moving to Rendsburg on 2 May. Some pilots flew to Norway to continue reconnaissance duties up to the end of the war, the last serviceable B-1s and B-2s being based at Stavanger.

21. An Ar 234 re-deployed at Stavanger, ostensibly to continue reconnaissance sorties but in reality as a means of safeguarding

the aircraft from the Allied advance. Together with some Ju 188s, about ten Ar 234B-1s and B-2s were captured at Stavanger by Norwegian and British forces at the end of the war, intact and quite airworthy. Other Ar 234B-1s, for example 140008, were stationed at Karup, and some of these were flown via Schleswig to No. 6 Maintenance Unit at Brize Norton by Lt. Cdr. E. M. Brown, a British specialist pilot who flew a large number of captured German and Italian aircraft.

22. This photograph was taken at Manching at the end of April 1945. In the damaged hangar stand Ju 88G-6 night fighters 620313 and 620557, together with an Ar 234B-2. This Arado was one of the *KG 76* aircraft which operated from south-west Germany in an attempt to delay the advance of the Allied ground forces, for example by making low-level attacks on bridges and railway targets in Bad Münster and Bad Kreuznach. Three or four of the jet bombers were normally engaged on these sorties, and on 21 March 1945 hits were claimed by pilots from the remnants of *6 Staffel, KG 76*.

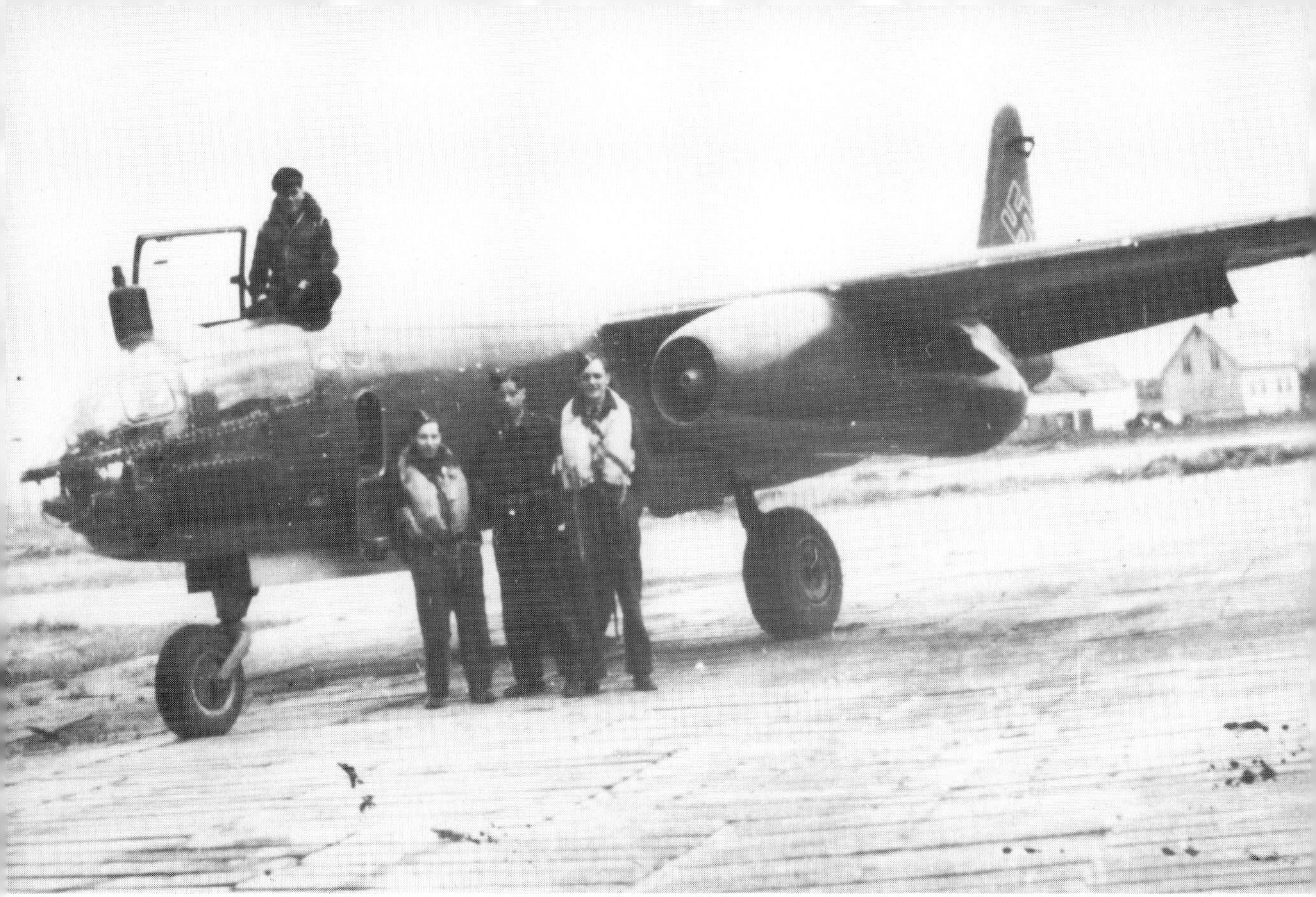

21▲ 22▼

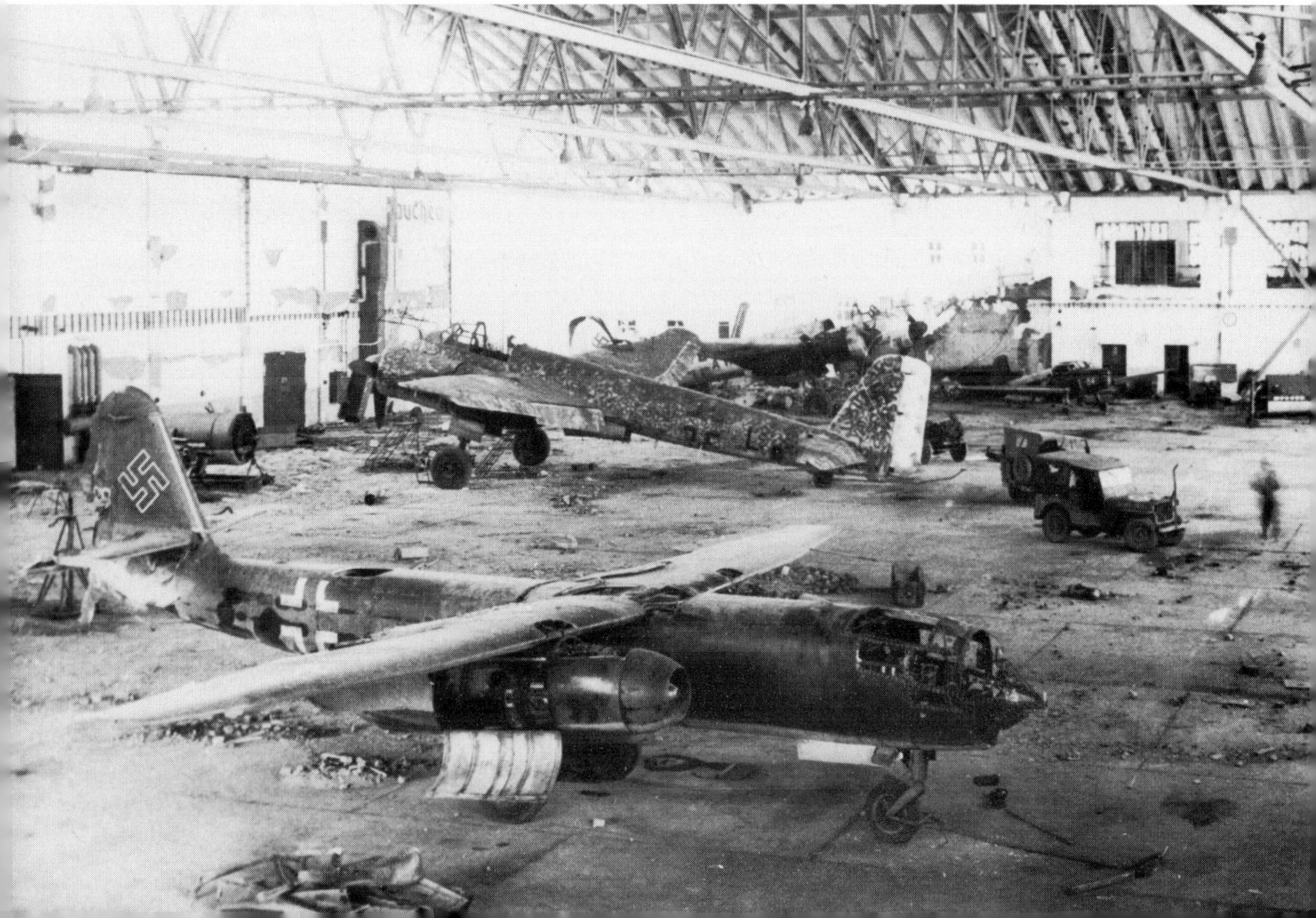

23. An Ar 234B-1 from *Kommando 'Sperling'* photographed shortly after take-off, early 1945. The unit, part of the *Aufklärungsgruppe* of *Luftwaffenkommando West*, was tasked with exploring enemy ground concentrations, flying its aircraft from forward bases in France and Belgium. Some of the reconnaissance aircraft assigned to *Kommando 'Sperling'* were equipped with two 300-litre drop tanks; the JATO units were jettisoned after take-off.

24. In addition to 140008, nine Ar 234B-1s and B-2s were flown by pilots of the RAF, most of the aircraft having been captured in northern Germany. The American forces found three Ar 234B-2s on airfields near Munich in bad condition, so they acquired two aircraft for Col. Watson's Operation 'Seahorse' from the British. These were flown by USAF pilots at Lechfeld in June 1945 and, together with an Me 262A-1, A-1/U3, B-1 and B-1/U1, were subsequently transferred via Melun to Cherbourg and taken to the USA aboard the British carrier *Reaper*.

25. The He 178 V1 (which differed from the second prototype in having a fixed undercarriage) first took to the air on 27 August 1939 at the hands of *Flugkapitän* Erich Warsitz, who managed the twelve successful flights made by this well-known German jet aircraft at Rostock-Marienehe. The experimental He 178 V1 was powered by the He S3A developed by Dr. Hans von Ohain, who designed his first gas turbine at Göttingen University in 1936. Von Ohain constructed the first eleven Heinkel jet engines, culminating in the He S11A. The latter was being manufactured, though in very limited numbers, at Zuffenhausen near Stuttgart early in 1945, it having been decided to adopted this powerful engine for the Ar 234, the Me 262 and the He 162A-1/A-2 'Volksjäger'.

26. The second prototype He 178 had a fully retractable undercarriage and an increased wing span, but after the *RLM* (*Reichsluftfahrtministerium*) abandoned the He S6 jet engine there was no more interest in the He 178 V2, and in fact it probably never flew.

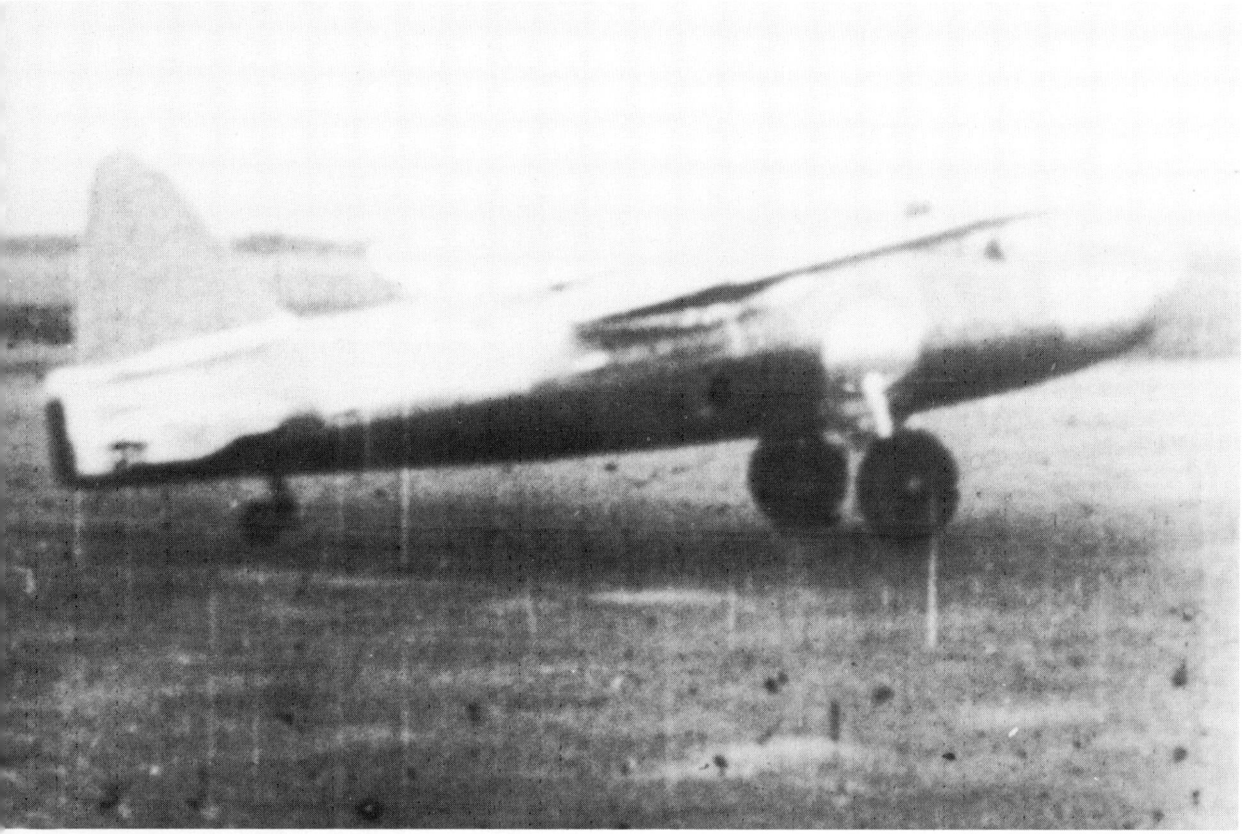

25▲ 26▼

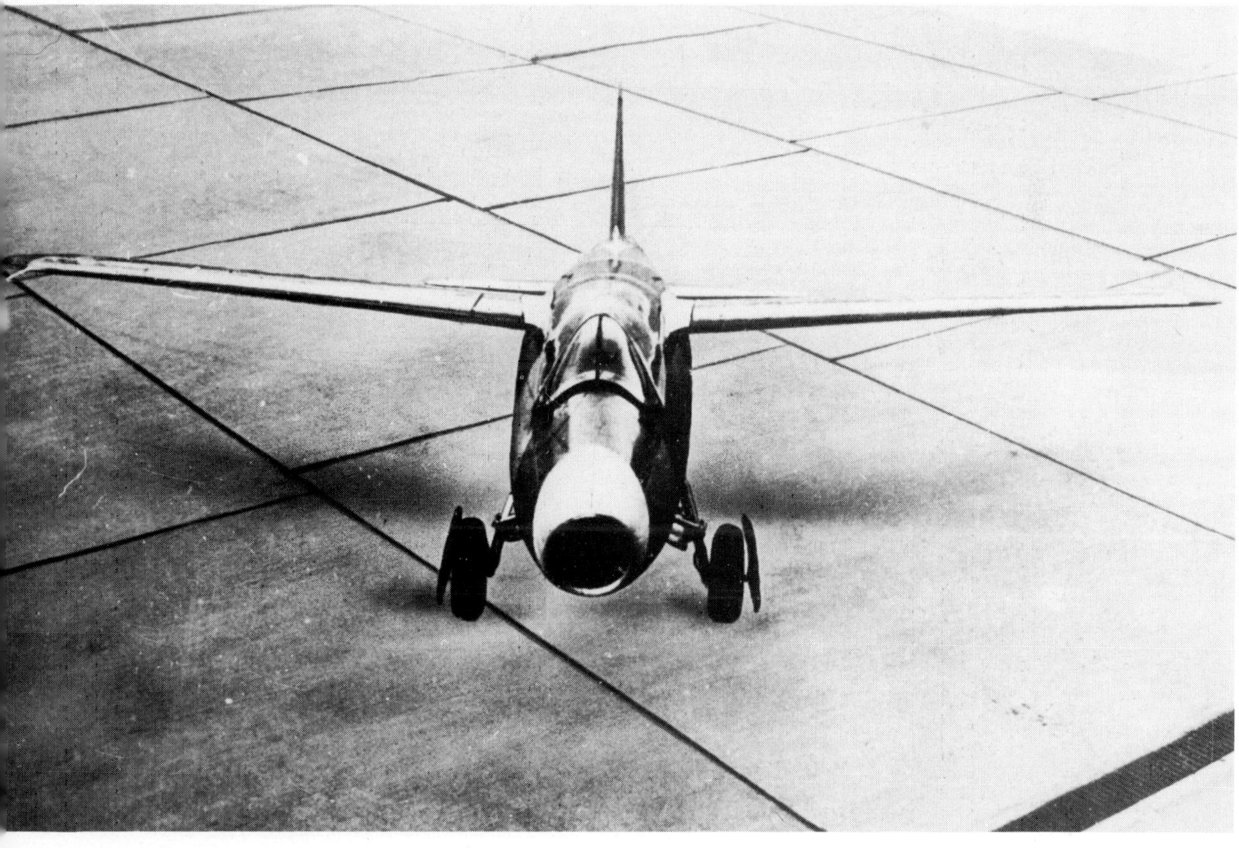

▲27

▲28　▼29

27. First take-off for the He 280 V2 (GJ + CA), which was flight-tested between 30 March 1941 and 26 June 1943 at Rostock-Marienehe and Wien-Schwechat. During the initial evaluation of the second He 280 the aircraft was propelled by two prototype He S8A engines. The first run produced a maximum thrust of only 500kg, although later, in 1943, 720kg would be attained. The engine cowlings were left off for the maiden flight in order to prevent overheating. The He 280 V2 was lost on 26 June 1943 in an accident caused by an engine failure.

28. The He 280 V2 received two Jumo 004 engines early in 1943 and completed its first flight with the new installation on 16 March. The 004 was also fitted to the He 280 V8 (NU + EC), which was flown for the first time on 19 July 1943. After some ten flights the V8 was used in 1944 as a second unpowered prototype to evaluate the new 'vee' tail for the 'Volksjäger' proposal. The photograph shows a Jumo 004B-1 engine.

29. The third He 280 prototype (GJ + CB) first took off on 5 July 1942 from Marienehe airfield near Rostock, with *Flugkapitän* Fritz Schäfer at the controls. The experimental jet fighter was equipped with two Heinkel He S8As, and by the end of 1942 had completed more than fifteen successful sorties, attaining a speed of 620kph during two flights each of 11 minutes' duration. The photograph was taken after a heavy landing near Lichtenhagen on 8 February 1943. Following a flame-out, Fritz Schäfer was unable to control the aircraft and was forced to make an emergency landing. The pilot was unhurt, and the aircraft was repaired within a few days.

30. A close-up view of the Heinkel He S8A turbine shows the compactness of von Ohain's design: the engine looks much smaller and lighter than the Jumo 004 (109-004) shown before. Only 32 of these powerplants were manufactured at the Heinkel works owing to a two-year delay in producing the promised thrust of 700kg, and then only two He 280s received the engine. The proposed He 280 V1 and V5 were never flown with Heinkel turbines. The He 280 V4 was completed in 1943 but did not fly: parts of this aircraft lay at Hörsching near Linz in October 1944, too badly damaged to join the detailed test programme.

31. The second Heinkel He 280, seen shortly before a test flight during the early stages of its development in 1941; there are still no codes on the fuselage. *General* Udet believed that the He 280 would become one of the *Luftwaffe's* front-line fighters after visiting the Heinkel works at Marienehe to observe the second flight of the He 280 V2. Udet never flew the He 280, but he was very enthusiastic about the new engine technology.

▲ 32   ▼ 33

32, 33. The He 280 V3 (plus some cyclists!) is towed by a little Hanomag truck at Rostock-Marienehe following one of Fritz Schäfer's flight tests. Schafer, together with Paul Bader, conducted most of the experimental flights at Rostock and Vienna. Prior to the cancellation of the He 280, plans existed for building more than 30 prototypes, but in April 1943 the quantity was reduced by the *RLM* to twelve, and later to only nine test-beds, which would cover the entire engine development programme and all the high-speed tests. By early 1945 the He 280 V7 had been hauled behind an He 111H-6 on well over 100 occasions!

34▲

34. One of the two mock-ups built at Rostock for testing three forward-firing MG 151/15 machine guns, an installation intended for the He 280A-1 and, after this was cancelled, for the BMW 003-powered He 280B-1. Heinkel later proposed a heavier armament consisting of 20mm and 30mm weapons, to be installed in the nose of his own jet fighters. The heaviest weapons system was proposed in December 1942 and consisted of an He 280B armed with three or possibly five MK 108s, each with 70 rounds.

35. The two Heinkel aircraft which did not get a real chance to prove themselves: the He 177 heavy bomber with its coupled DB 610 engines, and the unfortunate He 280 jet fighter, again a victim of mistakes by the *RLM* in their policy of engine procurement. After the victories of the first 'Blitzkrieg' there was no great interest in developing powerful aircraft engines, and when they were desperately needed it proved difficult to make up the lost time.

36. The He 280 V7 (NU + EB, also registered D-IEXM) was transferred to the *Deutsche Forschungsnstalt für Segelflug* for a series of aerodynamics trials at Ainring/Bavaria to compile data for new 'vee' tail surfaces proposed for high-speed jet aircraft, especially the He 162 'Volksjäger' and the 'Hochgeschwindigkeits Me 262'. The trials were conducted by test pilots Jan and Mohr in August and September 1944 by towing the V7 up to an altitude of 12,000–15,000ft behind *DFS* Heinkel He 111H-6 SS + KA.

35▲   36▼

▲37

37. The He 162 *'Volksjäger'* ('People's Fighter') was the subject of one of the *Luftwaffe's* desperate programmes aimed at countering the overwhelming production rates of Allied aircraft, but few of the aircraft produced under these programmes ever saw active service, thanks to the attacks mounted against production sites and air bases by British and US fighter-bombers. This He 162A-2 was hit and damaged on the tail; its jet engine has been removed for use in another *'Volksjäger'*.

38. The first production He 162 was completed at Berlin-Oranienburg on 24 March 1945, and by the end of the month mass-production had begun both here and at five other sites. However, the *'Languste'* underground factory near Mödling in Austria stopped work on 5 April when Allied ground forces reached the Vienna area, and a day later all activities at Schwechat came to an end. At the Mittelwerk near Nordhausen (Harz), *'Volksjäger'* production had begun at the end of March, only to be halted on 10 April, when the first parts were transferred to Bavaria.

39. This He 162A-2, the first to be built at Rostock-Marienehe, was rolled out for its maiden flight on 25 March 1945. Many

'Volksjäger' components were produced at Rostock-Theresienfeld, but, here again, both factories stopped work on 2 May. Most of *JG 1*'s He 162A-2s were manufactured at Rostock and later flown to Leck in northern Germany. Some of the aircraft were flown to Rechlin for a short but intensive series of trials, but after Rechlin was captured by Soviet forces *'Erprobungsstaffel 162'* moved to Memmingen in Bavaria, only to be disbanded a few days later.

40. Junkers were ordered to start He 162 production at Bernburg near Dessau, and on 24 March 1945 the first Junkers-built He 162A-2 was ready to fly. The company had in fact been working on high-speed fighter aircraft since November 1944, and at the *Abteilung 700* Junkers specialists and a few Messerschmitt designers were tooling up for Me 163 and Ju 248 production. Bernburg became part of the huge *'Volksjäger-Programm'*, itself a part of the *'Führernotprogramm'*, to which certain *Luftwaffe* aircraft and guided weapons projects were assigned. Soon after the first Junkers-built *'Volksjäger'* was completed, however, work came to an end because of a shortage of BMW 003 engines.

▼38

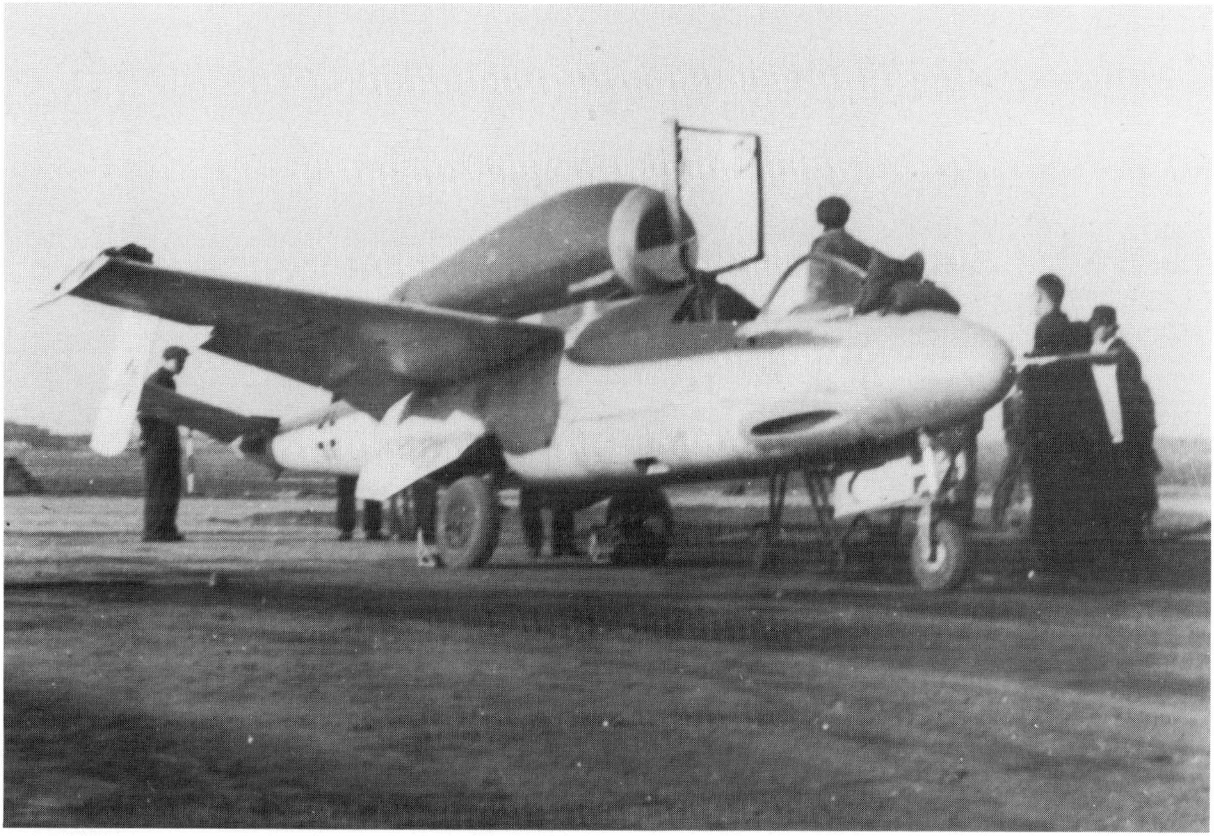

39▲ 40▼

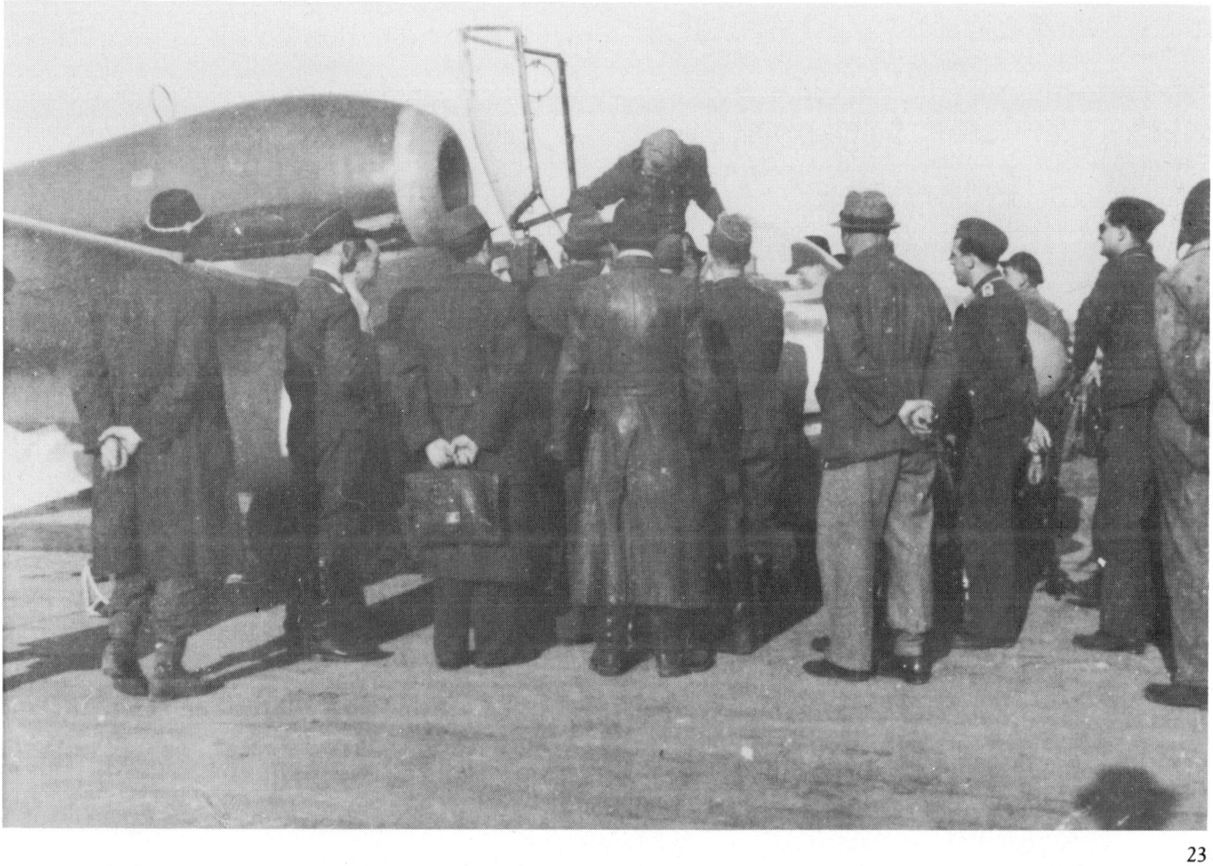

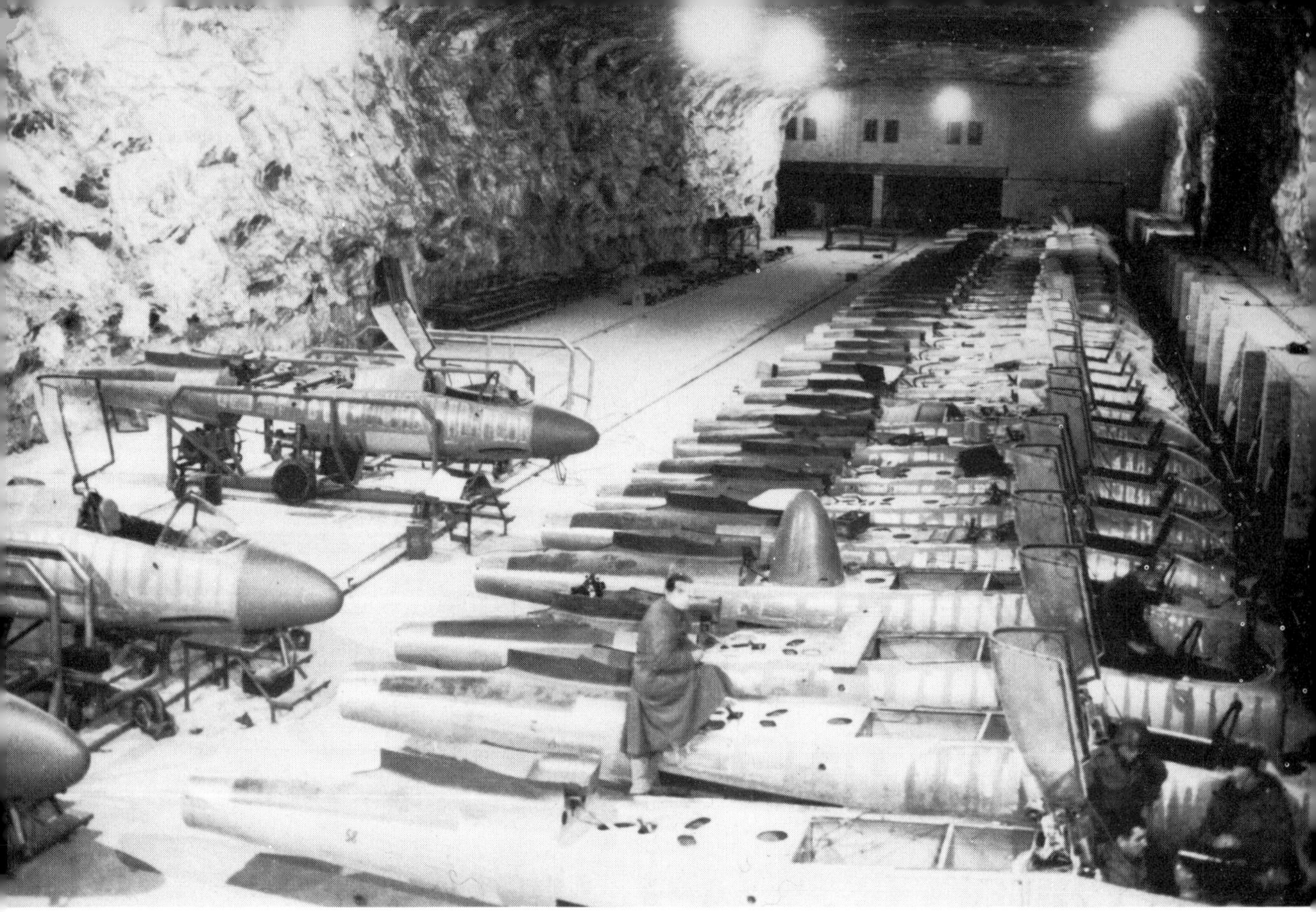

▲41 ▼42

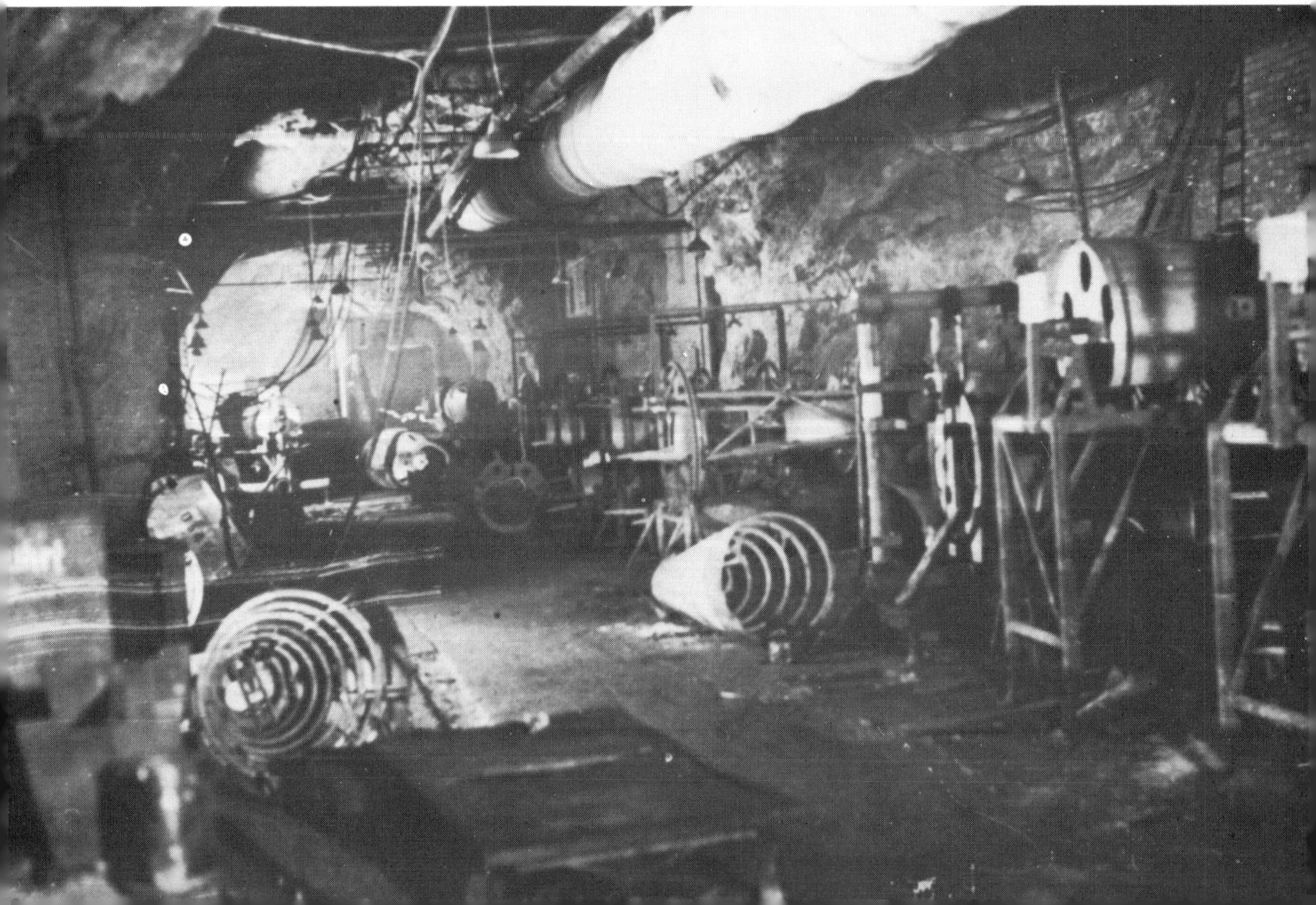

41. The underground He 162 production site near Eger following its occupation by the Allies at the end of the war. The first aircraft had been rolled out on 8 May 1945, and over 60 fuselages in an advanced state of completion were discovered. The effects of Allied air raids during 1944 and 1945 had forced German aircraft manufacturers to seek such rocky protection in order to continue production. Note, in this photograph, that several Allied soldiers have taken their seats in the unique 'Volksjäger'.

42, 43. Only fuselages for the 'Volksjäger' were built at the 'Languste' underground factory, but as the Allies closed in employees from the Heinkel works at Schwechat attempted to demolish the site with explosives, damaging many of the assemblies and most of the jigs and tools on both floors of the

complex. The SS then arrived from Vienna with orders to kill the slave workers, but many were saved by personnel from Heinkel. By May 1945 the site had been cleared of He 162 components and gypsum production was under way once more.

44. The last days of the 'Volksjäger's operational career: He 162A-2s of Einsatzgruppe JG 1 wait in line for the British ground forces at Leck. A few days after Erprobungskommando 162 had blown up its last aircraft at Memmingen – on 4 April 1945 – it was allowed to commence He 162 operations over the Reich, and at the end of April 1945 'Volksjäger' from I/JG 1 were trying to intercept low-flying Allied fighter-bombers over northern Germany. During the last days of the war the first and second Gruppen joined I(Einsatzgruppe)/ Jagdgeschwader 1 at Leck.

▲45

▲46   ▼47

45. A poor-quality photograph depicting what appears to be an He 162 two-seat training aircraft with a fixed undercarriage and no engine. Various trainer conversions were planned in October and November 1944, using different wing spans and fitted both with and without BMW 003E powerplants, together with some static mock-ups with functioning turbojets. It was also proposed to build an He 162 cockpit coupled to an electrically operated BMW 003, with loudspeakers relaying the engine noise. About three training aircraft were under construction at end of 1944, and on 28 March 1945 the first of them was ready to fly at Trebbin. A few days later, however, the whole conversion training programme was stopped, and the aircraft were destroyed to prevent their capture by Soviet forces.

46. A photograph of the Ho IX V1 taken during the final stages of its assembly early in 1944 at Göttingen. The aircraft comprised three main sections – the main section with the undercarriage and the cabin, and each outer wing panel. A take-off was first attempted on 1 March 1944, the aircraft being towed behind an He 45, but it failed because the tug was too small. However, on 5 March the Ho IX followed an He 111 up to 12,000ft. After its third flight the aircraft was taken to Oranienburg on April 20, and having survived an Allied air raid and some further demonstration flights it was returned to Göttingen.

47. The first prototype Horten Ho IX, which was assembled at the company's *Sonderkommando IX* in Göttingen under the direction of Walter and Reimar Horten. Except for the missing jet engines and the design of its undercarriage, the Ho IX V1 was similar to the second prototype. These aircraft were unique 'flying wing' fighter aircraft, and production machines were scheduled to equip the first *Staffeln* of *JG 400* in April 1945. Only a few prototypes were completed by the Horten brothers, however, and no production aircraft ever achieved operational status.

48, 49. Two more photographs of the first Ho IX, which made a crash landing on 25 March 1944 after the nose undercarriage broke away; test flights were continued after repairs had been effected. The V1 was captured by Allied troops at Polzen on 19 April 1945, having successfully completed stability trials at Oranienburg early in 1945 at the hands of *Oberleutnant* Heinz Scheidhauer.

48▲   49▼

▲50   ▼51

28

50. A photograph showing the second Ho IX prototype at Oranienburg prior to its maiden flight. The Ho IX V2 crashed on 26 February 1945 during its fourth flight, killing Horten test pilot *Feldwebel* Ziller. The 'flying wing' was propelled by two Junkers Jumo 004s (selected following the serious problems encountered by the BMW 003s originally proposed), the two air intakes for which can be seen as alongside the cockpit as the aircraft is brought into position by Oranienburg's *Luftwaffe* personnel. The V2 was due to be transferred to *JG 400* after flight trials had been concluded.

51. A close-up view of the third prototype Ho IX, the V3 (also known as the Gotha Go 229 V3), after it had been transferred to Wright AFB in the United States. The aircraft was of mixed construction, the frame and some outer panels being made from sheet steel and other parts of the centre-section from aluminium, while the outer wings were fabricated from plywood. The large nosewheel was taken from an He 177 bomber. Production Ho IXs were to be built by the Gotha concern, but only a few Ho IX prototypes were completed since Gotha's interest was concentrated on developing its own P.60 flying wing. The V3 is currently preserved at Silver Hill in Maryland and will possibly be restored over the next few years.

52. The sixth Ho IX prototype under construction at Gotha's factory at Friedrichsrode, 14 April 1945. The Horton brothers proposed an armament consisting of four MK 108s each with 90 rounds or two MK 103s with 140 rounds, but a third proposal, shown here, had two MK 108s in the starboard section and two Rb 50/18 *Reihenbildgeräte* (automatic reconnaissance cameras) beside the port Jumo 004 turbojet. None of the armed versions was realized or flown.

53. The Junkers *Entwicklungsflugzeug* EF 122 was one of the company's experimental designs for a jet-propelled heavy bomber and reconnaissance aircraft, the Ju 287. Four distinct variants were proposed, differing from one another in using single, paired or clusters of three turbojets. In 1943 Heinkel began work on a more conventional four-engined jet bomber, the P.1068, later redesignated He 343, the first components for which had been manufactured by the end of the war: construction of the first two prototypes had started during the summer of 1944, but work was abandoned in March 1945 in favour of greater capacity for the 'Volksjäger'.

52▲   53▼

▲54

54. The first Ju 287 was completed at Dessau and a successful maiden flight took place on 8 August 1944 at an airfield belonging to *Erprobungsstelle* Rechlin; eight days later the aircraft was flown at Brandis near Leipzig. One of the pilots was *Flugkapitän* Siegfried Holzbauer, who took off with rocket assistance from three Walter RI 501s. The twin nosewheel was fitted to the first prototype in an attempt to overcome taxying problems.

55. A photograph showing the Ju 287 V1 hidden in woodland near Brandis early in 1945; the engines have been removed for use in other aircraft, which accounts for the tail-down attitude.

56. The first prototype Ju 287 following its capture by US forces in May 1945 at Brandis. Some weeks earlier, the *RLM* had given permission for work to continue on advanced projects

until the '*Endsieg*', and Junkers engineers started to adapt the '*Versuchsmuster*' to take two BMW 003s under each wing. The Ju 287 V1 (RS + RA) was destroyed at the end of April 1945, but some sources indicate that the Ju 287 V2 was completed after the war by German personnel forced to work in the USSR.

57. Prototype drawings relating to the Ju 287 programme, new cabin mock-ups, complete instrumentation for the bomb bay and a new undercarriage were all captured by Soviet forces near Leipzig. Of great interest were documents concerning Junkers '*Entwicklungsflugzeuge*' (experimental aircraft) designated EF 125, 131 and 132 and featuring powerful new BMW or Jumo engines and forward-swept wings.

▼55

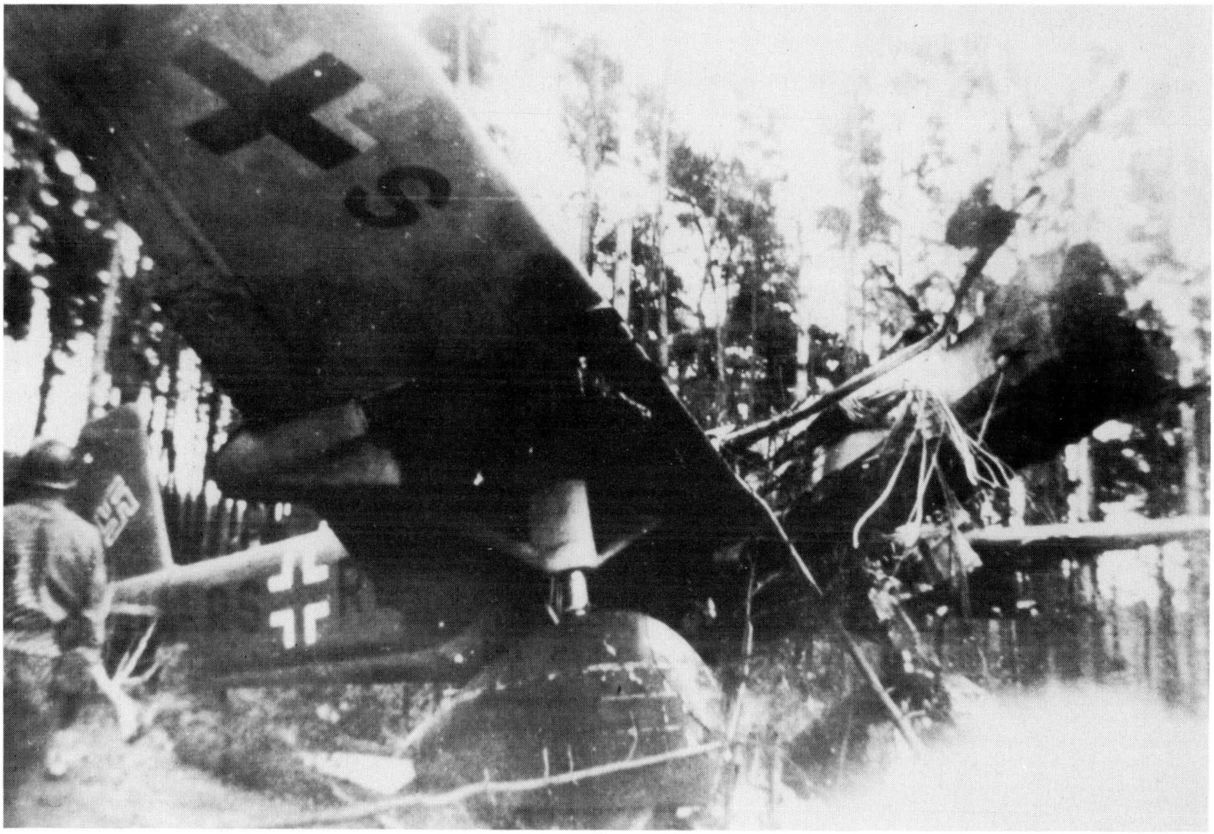

56▲ 57▼

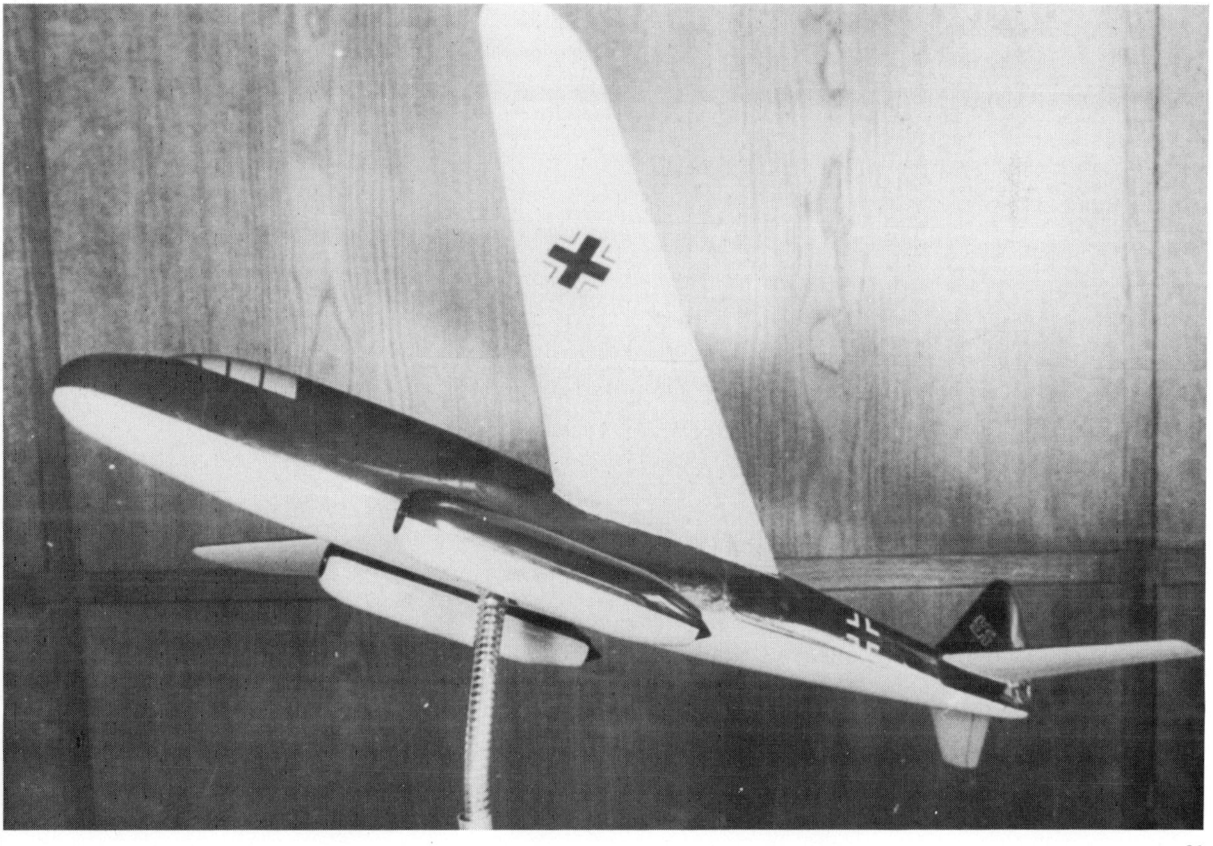

▲58

58. One of the models found at the Junkers plant showed a production version of the Ju 287 which was similar to the V2 prototype, propelled by six turbojets and armed with a remotely controlled weapon system at the tail consisting of two MG 151/20s in an FLH 151/z (*Zwilling*) mounting; the same weapons were proposed for the Ju EF 131 and EF 132 projects. The aircraft would have had a bomb bay capable of accommodating two 2,000kg bombs, four SC/PC 1000s or eight SC 500s. Alternatively, there was enough space for one Fritz X remotely controlled bomb or up to forty-eight SC 50s carried on newly designed bomb racks.

59. One of the many Junkers bomber projects never to be realized during the Second World War, the Ju EF 122B was under construction from about late summer 1943. Several wind-tunnel models were tested between 1943 and 1945 at Dessau, but because there were no means of actually building such large bomber aircraft the only legacies are fascinating drawings and models like this.

▼59

60. The Me 262 V1 (PC + UA) – seen here, to the left, beside a Bf 108 – was first flown on 4 April 1941, under the power of a Jumo 210G piston engine adapted from that installed in a Bf 109D. A contract for installing Jumo 004s under the wings of the new jet fighter was placed on 8 December that year, but their development took longer than was anticipated by the *RLM* specialists: the first Jumo 004 prototypes were tested in 1941–42, but nobody believed that the first Jumo T1 production turbojets would be available before mid-1942. Two experimental Jumo 004s were ready early in 1942, and the Me 262 V1 flew with these on 19 July that year.

61. The Me 262 V3 on the runway. The third prototype (PC + UC) was the first to be equipped with the new Jumo 004 (T1) and took off for the first time on 18 July 1942. The aircraft suffered damage on 11 August 1942 and 17 August 1943; an Allied air raid on the Messerschmitt factory on 9 September 1944 caused further (75 per cent) damage, following which the V3 was never repaired.

60▲   61▼

33

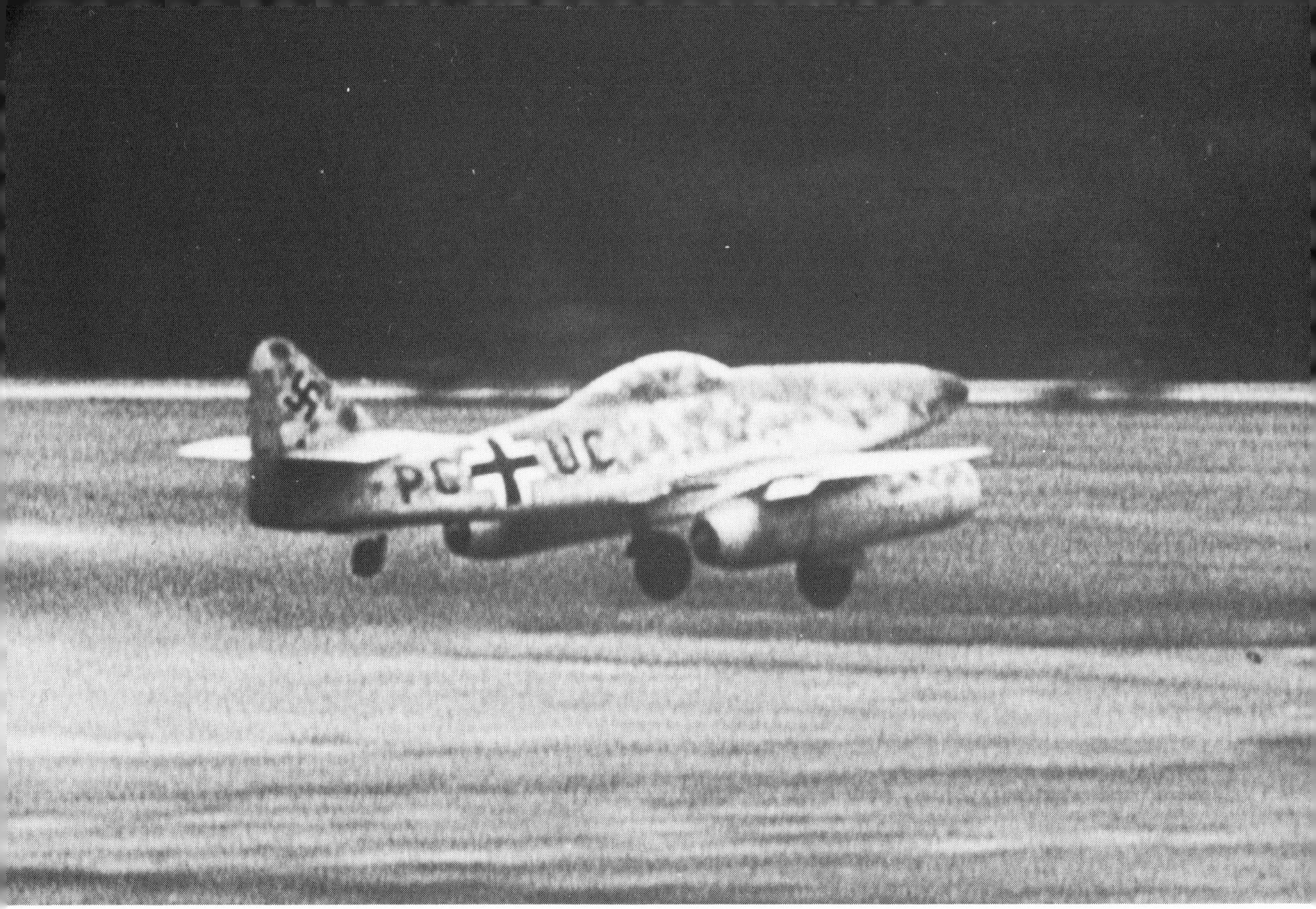

▲62 ▼63

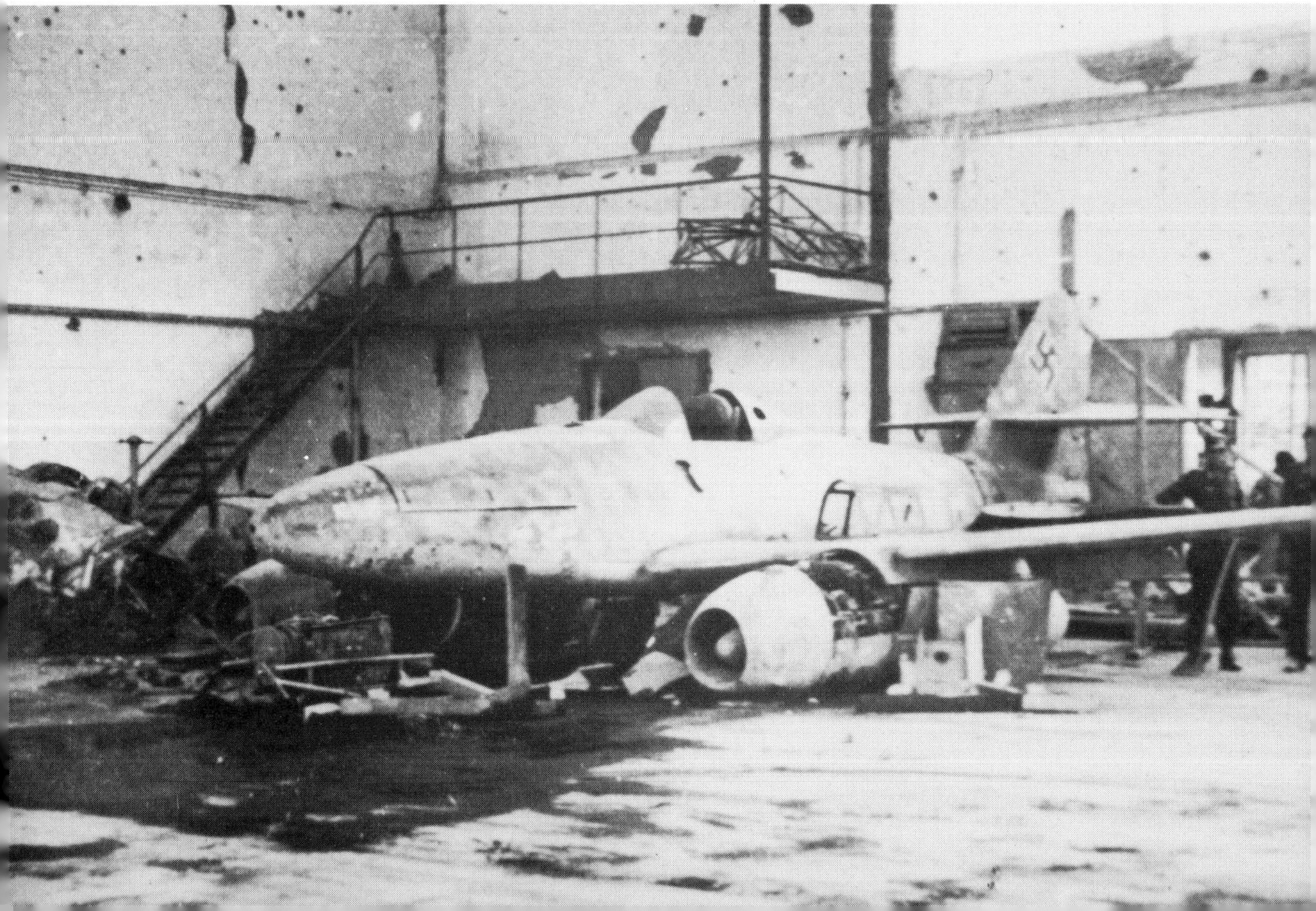

62. Fritz Wendel's first flight with the third Me 262 prototype at Leipheim in the early morning of 18 July 1942. The second flight took place at midday, after which it was decided to increase the size of the aircraft's wing roots in order to improve the airflow. After six flights with Fritz Wendel at the controls, Heinrich Beauvais flew the V3, but during his first take-off he did not achieve sufficient airspeed, the tail stayed down, and the aircraft was damaged during the subsequent tour of the cornfield at the end of the runway. Repaired, the aircraft was flown again on 20 March 1943.

63. A photograph taken at Lechfeld in 1944 and showing minor damage to an unidentified early Me 262 prototype. The print was found by a German soldier who was ordered by Allied NCOs to burn the private property of *Luftwaffe* personnel at a PoW camp in Bavaria in May 1945. The aircraft is apparently unarmed and differs from other early Me 262s in having a cockpit canopy of a new design.

64. The Me 262 V5 during one of its early flights over Lechfeld. The aircraft was used for trials aimed at shortening the long take-off phase by installing two Borsig RI 502 rocket packs. The additional thrust enabled the pilot to reduce the roll by about 300m, and a successful first flight was made on 7 June 1943. During a take-off on 4 August the nosewheel tyre burst, and following repairs the V3 flew with *Erprobungskommando 262*. It crashed on 1 February 1944.

65. The Me 262 S3 (VI + AH, *Werk Nr*. 130008) was the third series-production Me 262 fighter aircraft. On 16 April 1944 it suffered serious damage during a test programme as a result of one of the 262's many undercarriage failures. 'Red Three' was subsequently repaired and flew again, despite the fact that both Jumo engines had been torn off. The S3 was one of a series of fifteen aircraft, most of which were operated by *Erprobungskommando 262*, *Erprobungsstelle Rechlin-Lärz* and *1 Staffel* of *KG 51 'Edelweiss'* (the first jet bomber unit). Most of these aircraft were damaged during development testing, although a few were lost to Allied action.

66. The Me 262 V6 (VI + AA, *Werk Nr*. 130001) was the first prototype to be fitted with a fully retractable tricycle undercarriage and the second to be equipped with improved Jumo 004B-1s and refined cowlings; the aircraft, like many other early Me 262s, was painted pale blue-grey overall. It made its maiden flight on 17 October 1943 at Lechfeld with Lindner at the controls, *Oberst* Peltz flying the V6 in late December and evaluating the aircraft for its new '*Blitzbomber*' role. It was written off on 8 March 1943.

64▲

65▲   66▼

▲67   ▼68

69 ▲

67. The sixth Me 262 prototype, photographed at Lechfeld: the aircraft's wings are covered in woollen tufts for obtaining data about airflow patterns. Once its flight trials had been completed in October 1944 the aircraft was used for ground tests and for improving the brakes and the nose gear, but in spite of very many corrections and modifications, accidents caused by undercarriage failure continued to occur and many aircraft – on which the front-line units had been depending – had to be written off.

68. Another early Me 262 was VI + AB (*Werk Nr.* 130002), the V7 prototype, which started its flight trials on 20 December 1943 at Lechfeld. This aircraft survived two minor accidents on 21 February and 8 March 1944, again brought about by the undercarriage collapsing. Kurt Schmidt, the pilot, escaped unhurt and continued flight testing with another Me 262. The V7 was, however, severely damaged on 19 May 1944 and the aircraft was not apparently repaired.

69. Me 262A-1a 130167 was allocated the V5 prototype designation in the winter of 1944–45. Amongst its tasks were the testing of new brake systems and the proving trials of the EZ 42 gyroscopic gunsight, of which only a very few were fitted to *Luftwaffe* fighters during the last six months of the war. The Me 262A-1a was armed with four 30mm MK 108 guns each initially with 80 rounds although by early 1945 each of the upper guns could take 100 rounds. Me 262A-1s were equipped with the Revi 16D gunsight, although some *Schulflugzeuge* (training aircraft) had the older Revi 16B.

70. An Me 262A-1a assigned to *Erprobungskommando 262* at Lechfeld taxies for take-off. The first operational jet fighter unit, commanded by the well-known Bf 110 pilot *Hauptmann* Werner Thierfelder, flew sorties against high-flying Allied reconnaissance aircraft and heavily escorted bombers. Thierfelder was killed on 18 July 1944 when his Me 262 S6 (VI + AK, *Werk Nr.* 130011) was shot down by P-51s near Kaufering in Bavaria, and on 5 August 1944 *Hauptmann* Horst Geyer took over command.

70 ▼

71. *Major* Walter Nowotny, the *Luftwaffe*'s fifth highest scoring fighter ace (258 victories), who commanded the first operational Me 262 *Gruppe*, the so-called *Kommando 'Nowotny'*. The *Gruppe* achieved more than 45 victories, about a third of them after the *Kommando* had been withdrawn from the front line and re-trained on the 262. The unit later became an important part of *III/Jagdgeschwader 7*, whose first victory occurred on 25 July 1944 when *Lt.* Schreiber attacked a DH Mosquito over Bavaria and whose second concerned a Spitfire which failed to return from a sortie over the Stuttgart area in early August.

72. *Kommando 'Nowotny'* lost 26 Me 262A-1a fighters between 4 October and 11 November 1944. Only about five of the losses could be ascribed to enemy action: most of them came about as a result of take-off or landing accidents, some of the latter caused by the aircraft running out of fuel. The Me 262 shown here was found at Neubiberg in May 1945. It was one of the few A-1as of *Kommando 'Nowotny'* to survive the 1944 operations over north-west Germany. Behind it is a rarity – a Ju 88 with a standard A-4 fuselage but fitted with BMW 801 engines.

73. This poor-quality photograph is nevertheless a precious record of the operational career of *Jagdgeschwader 7* flying from bases in central Germany. 'Yellow Four' was one of the jet fighters of the famous *JG 7 'Hindenburg'*, which later became the officially named *'Nowotny'* after the leader of the first jet fighter unit to operate with the *Reichsverteidigung* was killed in action.

74, 75. Two photographs showing the demise of a B-24 Liberator under the guns of an Me 262A-1 belonging to *III/JG 7 'Nowotny'*: the wing and one engine of the bomber were set on fire, and the aircraft spun out of control. The Me 262A-1's armament consisted of four MK 108 cannon – a formidable and effective battery. It was planned later to remove these guns and fit a new armament of six MK 108s or a newly designed nose section carrying two MG 151/20s, two heavy MK 103s and two additional MK 108s, but only one or two Me 262s had been re-equipped by the time hostilities ceased.

▲71 ▼72

73▲

74▲   75▼

▲76

76. During March and April 1945 a number of Me 262s were stationed at Brandis, Junkers' airfield being used by several pilots from *Jagdgeschwader 7*. There was naturally great interest in the new Me 262A-1, and the hangar was well camouflaged with shrubs on its roof. Despite such precautions, however, most of sites at which German jet aircraft were stationed received frequent attention from Allied bombers.

77. In March 1945 a number of *KG 51*'s Me 262 *'Blitzbombers'* were stationed at Rhein-Main for operations against the Allied

▼77

ground forces advancing on the other side of the River Rhine. Some of the Me 262A-1a/Bos and A-2as formerly belonged to *I Gruppe* of *KG 51 'Edelweiss'*, which saw service mainly over north-west Europe: *3 Staffel*, which recorded 58 missions during September 1944 alone, was particularly active. Later *3/KG 51* became part of a larger *Einsatzkommando KG 51* under the authority of *'Gefechtsverbana Hallensleben'*, which also included *Einsatzgruppe KG 51*, *III/KG 51*, *Nachtschlachtgruppen 1* and *2* and part of *III/KG 3*.

78. Also assigned to the celebrated *Kampfgeschwader 'Edelweiss'* were these Me 262s. During February and March 1945 most of the *'Blitzbomber'* missions undertaken by *KG 51* were flown against Allied concentrations behind the front line; others consisted of attacks like that on the bridge at Remagen, involving 25 Me 262 bombers, and low-level bombing raids against targets near Bad Kreuznach and Bad Münster am Stein. Few such sorties were made after the middle of March 1945.
79. Me 262s parked at the edge of dense woodland alongside the former Ulm–Augsburg–Munich Reichsautobahn. Straight sections of the autobahn near Munich and Lübeck were used as improvised airstrips for jets assigned to *11/NJG 11 (Kommando 'Welter')* and *JV 44 (Jagdverband 44 'Galland')* in April 1945, but few missions were flown from these temporary sites owing to the limited availability of fuel, ammunition and spare parts. Most of these aircraft were left in bare metal finish because there was no time and little paint to camouflage them during the closing weeks of the Second World War.

▲80

80. A close-up view of one of the hidden German jets, lacking powerplants and of no practical value. This is an Me 262A-1a/Bo, equipped with so-called '*Wikingerschiff*' racks for mounting either bombs or auxiliary fuel tanks. As well as the Jumo 004B engines, the wheels, cockpit canopy and armament access panels are all missing. The structural integrity of the Me 262 airframe was inferior to that of the Bf 109 fighter, and flame-outs and other problems caused by the new engines further reduced the effectiveness of the aircraft.

81. A row of Me 262A-1as during final assembly at the secret '*Waldfabrik*' near Augsburg where an estimated 150 aircraft were to be produced. The actual output amounted to some 130 machines, most of them unserviceable because important fittings were not forthcoming from Obertraubling, Kitzingen, Leipheim, Neuburg or Schwäbisch-Hall where the majority of Me 262s were manufactured, generally under very difficult circumstances. The final assembly lines at Neuburg and Memmingen came to assume great importance during March and April 1945 because most of the other factories had been hit in Allied air raids and either partly or totally destroyed.

82, 83. Two photographs of the '*Waldmontage*'. Despite the extensive camouflaging of tents and workshops at Obertraubling, in February and March 1945 approximately sixty Me 262s were destroyed or severely damaged by Allied bombing, and the raid on Leipheim in late March put more than thirty airframes out of commission. Thereafter the highways and hidden factories became much more important. Near Lechhausen, *Hauptmann* Talk enlisted the help of the *Luftwaffen-Baubataillone* (*Luftwaffe* construction battalions) in an effort to complete the auxiliary factory as quickly as possible.

▼81

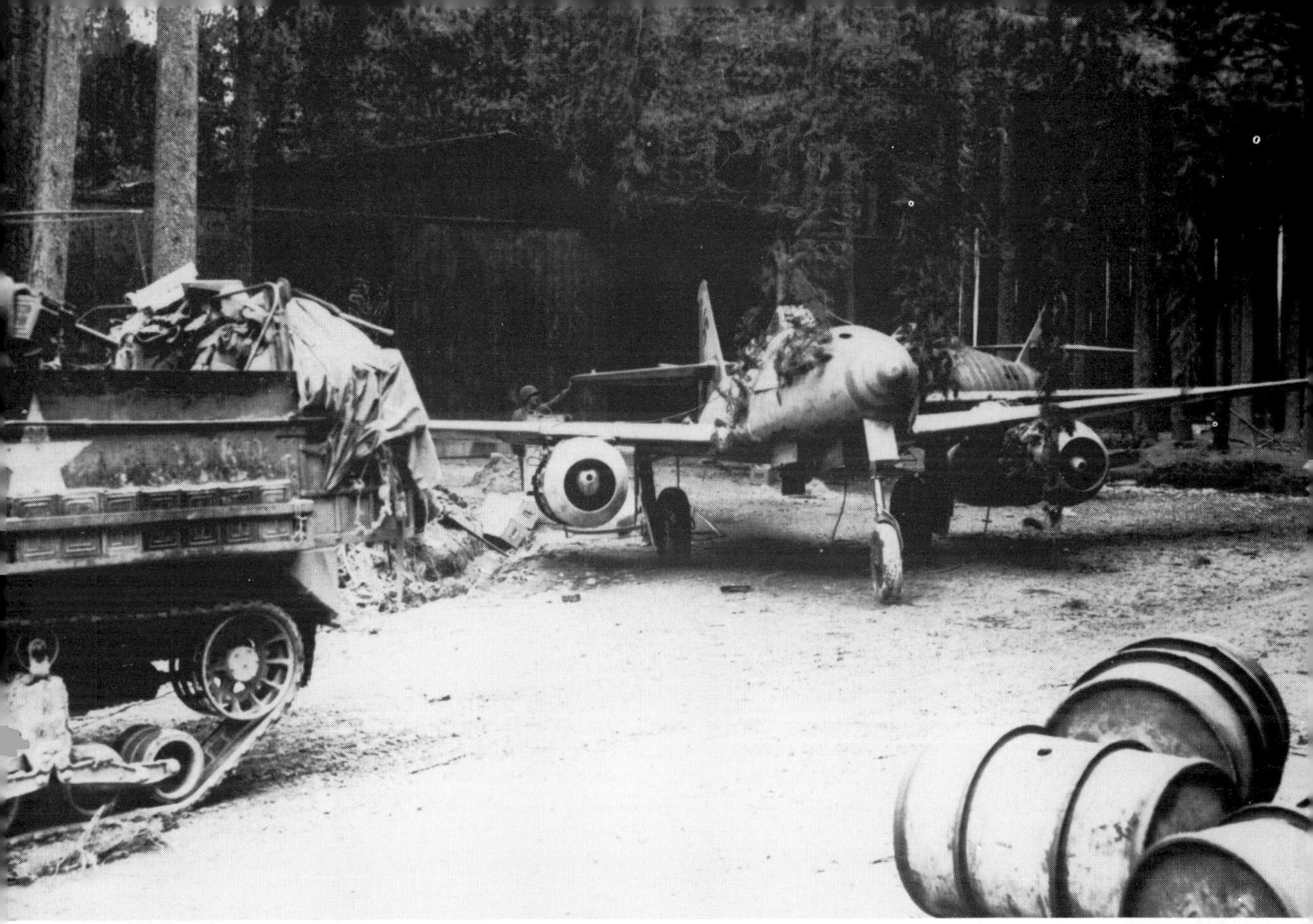

82▲ 83▼

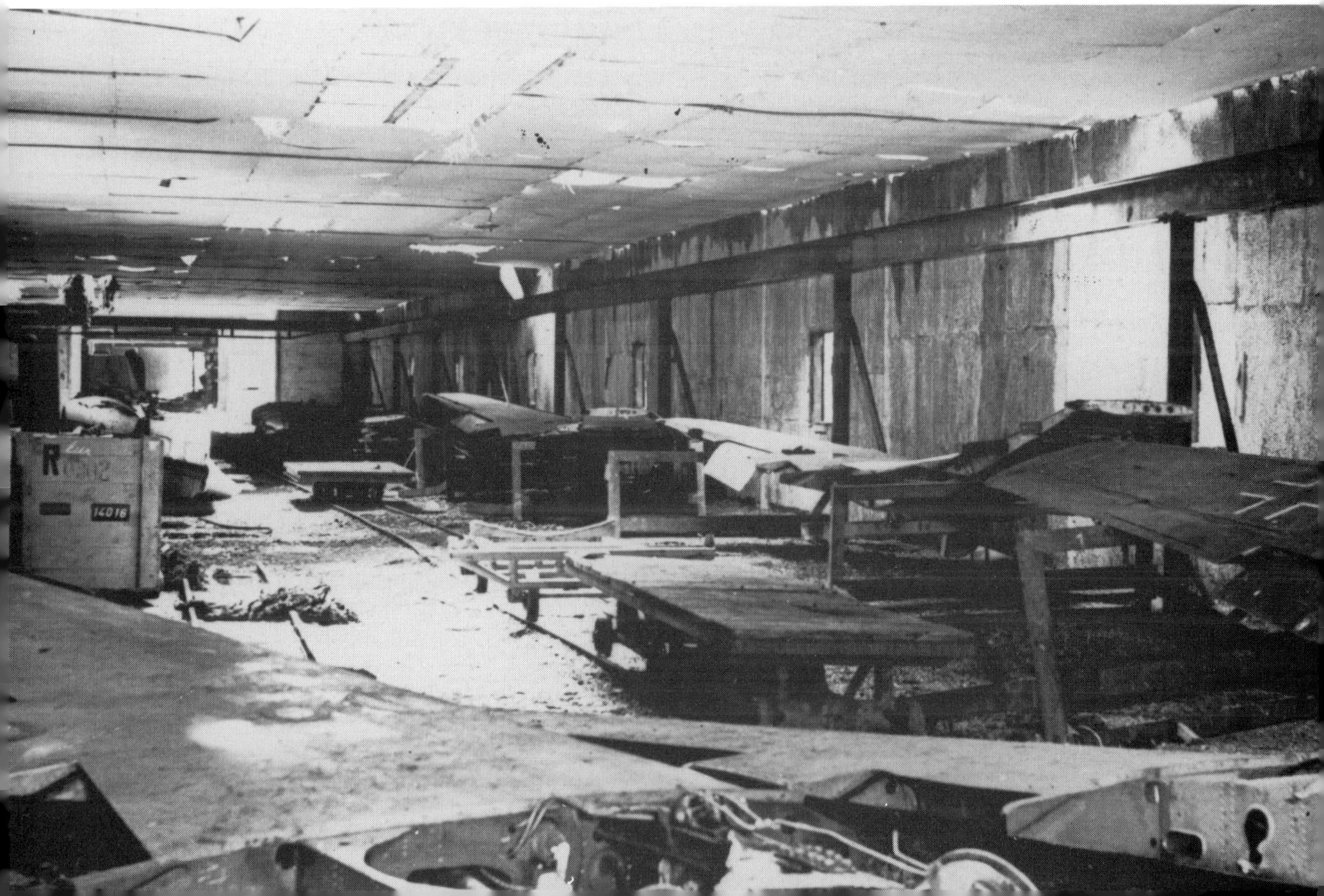

▲84

84. An Me 262A-1a/Bo which was completed before conditions reached their worst. The *Werknummer* 111603 belonged to the batch of aircraft built at Leipheim. Allied air reconnaissance located the dispersed assembly line, and the site was the target of a fighter attack in mid-November 1944. Fourteen out of 20 completed Me 262s were damaged as a result.

85. The airfield at Giebelstadt after concentrated bombing by the USAAF on 22 March 1945. The large hangar was

completely destroyed and a second was badly damaged by fire. Ninety Liberator bombers using 1,000lb bombs destroyed one Ju 88, only two Me 262s (nine others were damaged) and two Bf 109 fighters: 68 Me 262s which had been moved into the woods around the airfield escaped unscathed. Although the attack left about 200 craters on the runway, only two German soldiers were killed and seven wounded.

▼85

86. Two *'Blitzbombers'* of *KG 51 'Edelweiss'* at Rheine early in 1945. Ground crews strove to maintain as many jets as they could, under near-impossible conditions: large hangars were often hit by bombs and could not be used, and Me 262s in need of repair were frequently serviced in tents obtained from the great breweries of southern Germany.

87. Following conversion training at Lechfeld, the operational phase for most Me 262 pilots began early in 1945. General training started with a briefing, *III(Erg)/JG 2* giving the pilots theoretical instruction in the function and operation of jet engines. The men got more practical experience by using a wingless mock-up (which was also used for *'Volksjäger'* training), but the whole course was less than thorough and when they transferred to real aircraft accidents were common. Repairs were hampered by the unavailability of spare parts.

▲ 88

▲ 89   ▼ 90

88. An Me 262 jet fighter taxies to the runway at a central German airfield in 1945. The remnants of the first and second *Gruppen* of *JG 7* were partially absorbed by *Jagdverband 'Galland'*, to which some of the jet aircraft were handed over in late April that year, and many of the crewmen joined with the *Luftwaffenfelddivisonen* in ground battles in Lower Bavaria.

89. *Jagdgeschwader 7 'Nowotny'* saw action from virtually every airfield in central Germany. 'Yellow Seven', shown here, once belonged to *Kommando 'Nowotny'*. The gun camera has been taken away by someone as a souvenir, while the engine panels have been removed to allow the new technology to be inspected. The GI sitting in the cockpit is obviously pleased with life!

90. Few missions were flown by the Me 262 instructors of *KG 51*, *KG(J) 54*, *III(Erg)/JG 2* and *II/JG 7* since conversion training was interrupted by further Allied air attacks, for example the raid on 19 March 1945 by 125 heavy bombers of the 8th Air Force which hit Neuburg and destroyed fifteen or more of *KG(J) 54*'s Me 262s. Two days later 366 15th Air Force B-24s, escorted by 201 P-51 fighters, dropped over 800 tons of bombs on the airfield, which was totally obliterated.

91, 92. The seventh Me 262 bomber prototype, *Werk Nr. 170303*, was fitted with a pair of '*Wikingerschiff*' bomb racks beneath the forward fuselage to test the aircraft's suitability for carrying 500kg GP bombs and other payloads. Trials included the release of two SC 500 bombs from an altitude of 2,700ft and at a speed of about 700kph. Note the 1,000kg Borsig RATO gear beneath the fuselage. Tests with the two 1,000kg RATO units and a 1,000kg bombload were conducted during December 1944, and a RATO failure caused some minor damage to the aircraft in February 1945, but the Me 262 V7 was repaired at Lechfeld the following month.

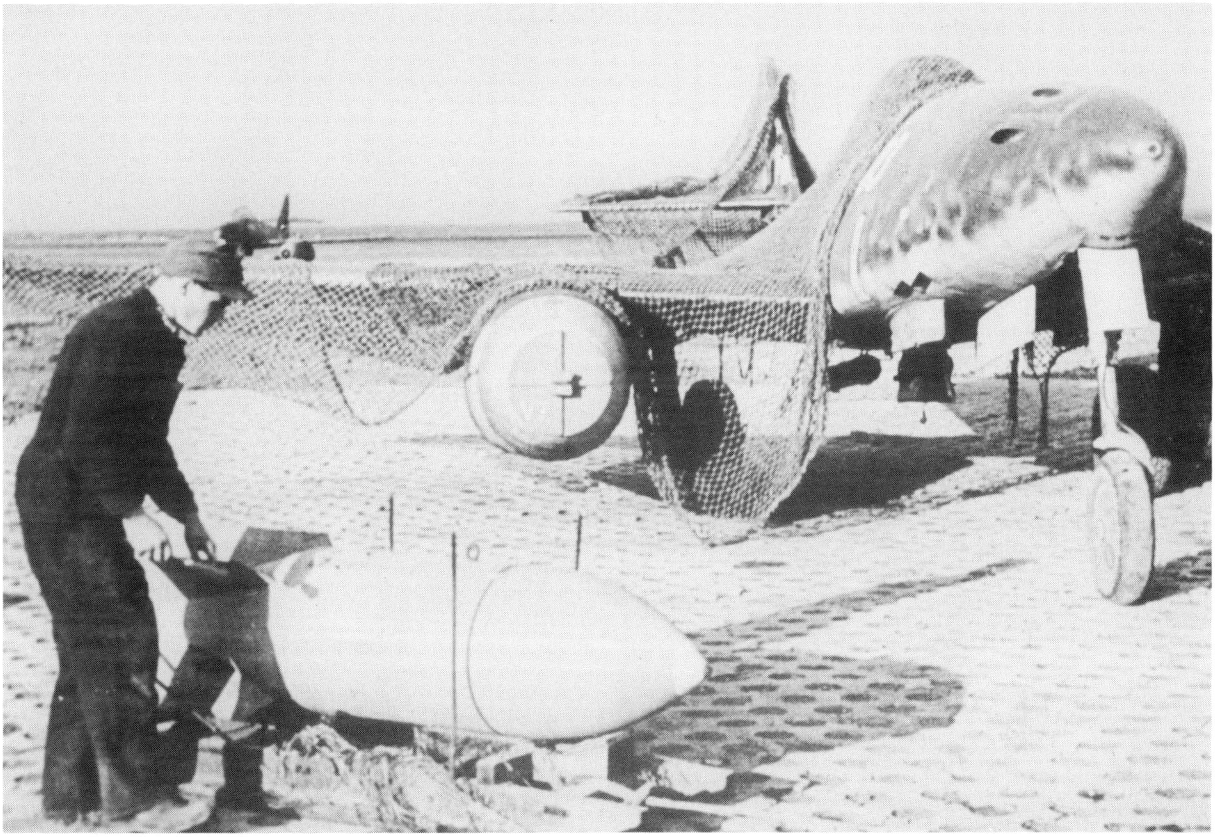

91▲ 92▼

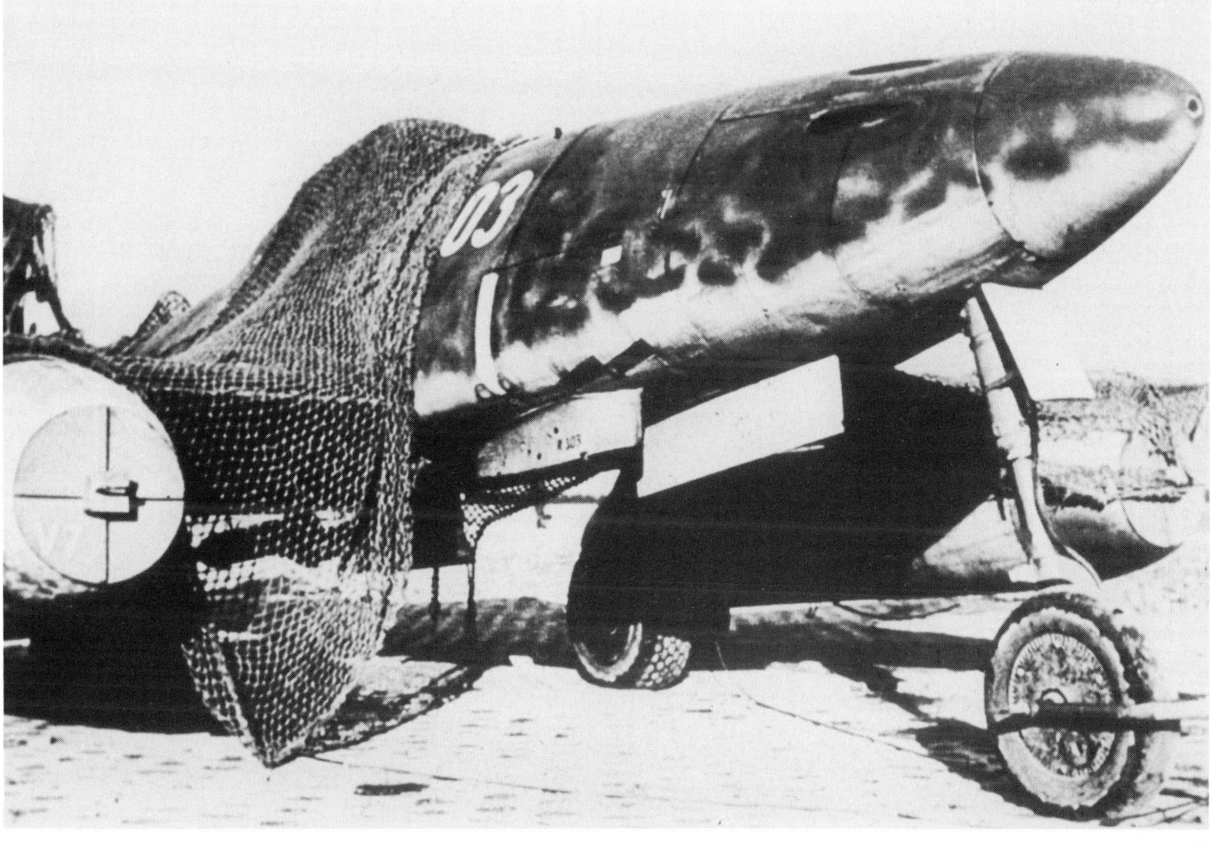

▲93

93. An Me 262A-2, *Werk Nr.* 170058. Three types of bomb rack could be fitted to Me 262s: the Schloss 503A-1 for 250 or 500kg bombs; the ETC 504A-1, used for carrying the BT 700 *bombtorpedo* anti-shipping weapon; and the '*Wikingerschiff*' racks, developed to carry the 500kg GP bomb or equivalent payload.

94. Toting a pair of 250kg GP bombs, Me 262A-1a/Bo 110813 waits for some action with *Kommando 'Schenk'* during the

winter of 1944–45. The *Luftwaffe* used the Me 262 to try out many novel types of ordnance, for example the AB 250 and 500, filled with 25 SD 15 or 84 SD 3 or 4000 incendiary pellets ('*Brandtaschen*'), used operationally against Allied bomber formations by aircraft of *Kommando 'Stamp'*. This air-to-air bombing was not successful, however, and the *Kommando* was disbanded, later becoming a component of *Jagdgeschwader 7*.

▼94

95. All Me 262 '*Blitzbombers*' sporting large, white-outlined, red code letters belonged to *Kommando 'Schenk'*, which was formed in June 1944 under the command of *Major* Wolfgang Schenk. The following month its first twelve pilots left Lechfeld, having only four hours' experience of flying the Me 262, for Chateaudun in France with nine aircraft. *Einsatzkommando 'Edelweiss'* had to withdraw to Creil by mid-August, then seven days later back to Juvincourt, and on 28 August to Ath-Chievres. Just two days after this a few of the aircraft took off to for Volkel-Eindhoven, but an Allied raid on this airfield forced yet another withdrawal to Rheine in early September.

96. From Rheine (where this photograph was taken), *Einsatzkommando 'Edelweiss'*, now known as *3(Einsatz)/Kampfgeschwader 51*, flew ground attack sorties against the Allied forces in Western Europe. Between 18 September and 1 October 1944, 58 missions were undertaken, only three of them aborted because of engine failure. After a period of bad weather in late September, *3/KG 51* flew 163 bombing missions in October 1944, resulting in the loss of five Me 262s, with one damaged and two others 'missing in action'. Most of the losses were attributable to Allied fighter activity.

▲97

97. An Me 262A-1a/Bo is loaded with two SC 250 bombs by its ground crew. In November 1944 *KG 51*'s jet bomber force consisted of 30 aircraft, of which 26 were serviceable, with 48 trained pilots. Most of the missions called for the use of AB 250s, but some attacks were made using SD 250 bombs. During the attack against Allied airfields on 2 November 1944, Hauptmann *Winkel* of *3/KG 51* made contact with fourteen enemy fighters, but despite receiving hits in the cockpit area Winkel succeeded in returning to Rheine to continue the raids against targets in Belgium and the Netherlands.

▼98

98. During the Ardennes offensive in December 1944, *KG 51* jet bombers flew their first mission six days after German ground forces had begun their attack, conducting a number of low-level sorties. *I/KG 51* subsequently took part in Operation '*Bodenplatte*', a large-scale raid against important Allied air bases in Western Europe. The Me 262 bombers joined about 800 piston-engined fighters and attacked the airfields near Eindhoven and Hertogenbosch. Among the casualties was *Oberfeldwebel* Erich Kaiser, shot down near Lingen.

99 ▲

99. The hard work of the ground crew: a weapons mechanic completes the fitting of an SC 250 GP bomb under the '*Wikingerschiff*' rack of a '*Blitzbomber*'. After attacking targets near Jülich and Kalkar, Me 262s from *KG 51* flew bombing missions against the bridge at Remagen between 7 and 18 March 1945. Early in April the unit had to move southwards because Allied ground forces had arrived in the Münsterland, and it was based successively at Giebelstadt, Kitzingen and Leipheim. The *Luftwaffe* command then ordered the transfer of most of the jet bombers to *Jagdgeschwader 7*.

100. The remains of *Oberst* Steinhoff's Me 262A-1a after his crash on 18 April 1945 when his aircraft hit the ground during a take-off at Munich-Riem. After successfully building up the *Stab* and *Stabsschwarm* of *JG 7* at Brandenburg as commanding officer in November 1944, he fell out with *Reichsmarschall* Göring and had to hand over command to *Major* Weissenburger on 14 January 1945. Johannes Steinhoff joined *General* Galland's *Jagdverband* and shot down six enemy aircraft before the war ended.

100 ▼

▲101

101. The sole Me 262C-1a '*Heimatschützer I*' (*Werk Nr.* 130186) took off from Lechfeld for the first time on 27 February 1945, using RATO gear; subsequent flights were made by Baur and Lindner, also from Lechfeld. In the closing stages of the war *Major* Heinz Bär of *III(Erg)/Jagdgeschwader 2* flew the aircraft on interception missions against Allied fighters: on one such flight, after the Me 262 had climbed to 27,000ft in only three minutes, a well-aimed burst of gunfire destroyed a P-51. After the war the rear fuselage of the C-1a was taken to Farnborough for examination by RAE experts.
102. Few Me 262 reconnaissance aircraft saw active service

with the *Luftwaffe*, despite the fact that the first Me 262 reconnaissance specifications were drawn up as early as 1941. Mock-ups were manufactured early in 1942, but the first Me 262A-1a/U3, *Werk Nr.* 170006, was not completed until August 1944. Two months later *Kommando 'Braunegg'* was established, to evaluate the Me 262 for the reconnaissance role. A few early Me 262A-1a/U3s were handed over, and in due course *Nahaufklärungsgruppe 6* flew the aircraft operationally in the West alongside Ar 234s. The surviving Me 262 reconnaissance jets were captured by the Allies at Lechfeld airfield.

▼102

103. Aircraft 170056 was the first Me 262 to be used for evaluating FuG 218 and FuG 226 '*Erstling*' early in 1945, but there is no evidence that this experimental fighter was ever flown in anger. A number of Me 262B-1a trainers were subsequently converted into two-seat night fighters by Deutsche Lufthansa at Berlin-Staaken. Antenna-equipped Me 262s were flight-tested by Baur, Lindner and Hofmann in February and March 1945, and it was discovered that the aerials became bent by the airflow at a speed of about 900kph.

104. Very few Me 262B-1 two-seat training aircraft were built, notwithstanding the real need for such aircraft. The Me 262B-1a was a conversion of the Me 262A jet fighter, and almost all the jet-equipped *Luftwaffe* units operated some. *III (Ergänzungs)/Jagdgeschwader 2* was established for fighter pilot conversion training in October 1944, with the promise that 122 Me 262A-1s and B-1s would be made available to that *Gruppe*, but, in the main, it was repaired Me 262A-1as that were flown at Lechfeld where *III(Erg)/JG 2* resided.

104▼

▲105 ▼106

105, 106. Two views of the cockpit interior of one of the five Me 262B-1a/U1 night fighters, which were coded 'Red 8' to 'Red 12' and bore the production numbers 170305, 170306, 110635, 110639 and 111980. All five aircraft reportedly saw action with *Kommando 'Welter' (10/NJG 11)*. *Oberleutnant* Kurt Welter, who was killed a few years after the end of the Second World War, scored more victories than any other German jet fighter pilot, with 28 confirmed and some probables, most of them Mosquitoes or Allied heavy bombers.
107. By far the majority of Me 262 missions were flown by day fighter pilots. 'White 13' belonged to *III/JG 7* and was operational until early 1945. During this time *III Gruppe* was stationed at Brandenburg-Briest near Berlin with 45 Me 262A-

1s, of which 80–85 per cent were normally serviceable, despite the difficult conditions during the last five months of the war. Losses, other than those inflicted by enemy action, could mainly be ascribed to engine failure (40 per cent), undercarriage problems (20), or pilot error (20).
108. The Me 262A-1a depicted in this photograph was one of the first jets delivered to *III Gruppe* and took part in the last desperate missions flown by *Jagdgeschwader 7*. On 10 April 1945 the *Geschwader*'s staff flight had five Me 262s on strength, 41 were flown by *I/JG 7*'s pilots, and a further 30 were operated by *III Gruppe*; *II/JG 7* did not fly its own aircraft until the final weeks of the war.

▲109

109. On 25 April 1945, Me 262A-1 'White Three' landed at Dübendorf in Switzerland, having spent its last drop of J2 fuel. The aircraft, *Werk Nr.* 500071, belonged to the 9th *Staffel* of *JG 7*, and at the controls was *Fähnrich* H. G. Mutke, who was interned by the Swiss authorities after interrogation. Years later the aircraft was handed over to the Deutsches Museum at Munich, where, following an expensive restoration, it is now a major attraction.

110. An Me 262A-1a belonging to the training unit *III(Erg)/JG 2* at Lechfeld in 1945 under the command of *Oberstleutnant* Bär, who with *Lt.* Schumacher flew many sorties over southern Germany. About ten instructors took part in those missions, and more than 30 air victories were scored, some of the men being awarded the Iron Cross (*Eisernes Kreuz*, or '*EK*') for their achievements.

▼110

111▲

111. An Me 262A-1a of *Jagdverband 'Galland'* during the unit's move to the Innsbruck area early in May 1945 after the last attacks against the medium bombers of the 15th Air Force had been mounted. Bär shot down about fifteen enemy aircraft during his time with *Jagdverband 'Galland'*, including five B-17s or 24s and five B-25s or 26s, on one occasion when flying the Me 262C-1a interceptor. Heinz Bär, whose victories totalled 200, was killed on 28 April 1957 when his light aircraft suddenly spun into the ground from an altitude of only 50m.

112. An Me 262A-1a found by Allied ground forces at Erding airfield in May 1945. It is not known to which unit this damaged fighter belonged, but there is some evidence that it was assigned to *JV 44 'Galland'*. On 28 April a proposal was made to withdraw the *Jagdverband* to Prague-Ruzin after the main elements of *JG 7* and the last aircraft of *KG 51* had been ordered there. Since American forces had moved in the direction of Munich by late April 1945 there was no chance of the unit retreating to improvised airstrips on the *Reichsautobahn* between Munich and Salzburg.

112▼

▲113 ▼114

113. US officers inspect the remains of an Me 262A-1a discovered in a hangar at the heavily bombed Messerschmitt works at Obertraubling in Bavaria. The aircraft had at one time been flown by members of *JV 44*. The unit shot down two B-26 Marauders and one P-51 Mustang during its first mission on 24 April, for the loss of one aircraft. During a second sortie, five Me 262A-1as of the *Jagdverband* tried to destroy a formation of Marauders en route to bomb targets in Bavaria, and *Oberst* Lützow was shot down.

114, 115. One of the few Me 262A-1as of *Jagdverband 44 'Galland'* which managed to escape to the Innsbruck area; the aircraft shows the typical camouflage scheme of *JV 44*'s machines. No missions were flown from Innsbruck because it proved impossible to finish work on the airfield. The last major sortie by *JV 44* had been flown at about 1100hrs on 26 April 1945 (only a few days before this photograph was taken), when its aircraft took off to intercept a formation of B-26s. *General* Galland identified the Marauders, pulled up to fire his cannon and one aircraft exploded. A second B-26 escaped because Galland had problems with his R4M rocket armament.

116. The end of the Me 262: Schwäbisch-Hall airfield during May 1945. At the end of the runway the remains of an Me 262A-1a, possibly 112249, lie discarded. The airfield was hit by Allied air attacks during the closing weeks of the war with the object of paralysing the activities of the German jets. Most of the remaining ground-attack Me 262s were handed over to *JV 44*, and the last examples, ten or twelve in number, were ordered to fly from Bavaria to Prague where they formed a *Gefechtsverband* with the pilots of *Jagdgeschwader 7, KG(J) 54* and *KG(J) 6*. *IX Fliegerkorps(J)* at Prague was meanwhile ordered by the *Luftwaffenführungsstab* to fly missions against advancing Soviet forces near Berlin.

115▲ 116▼

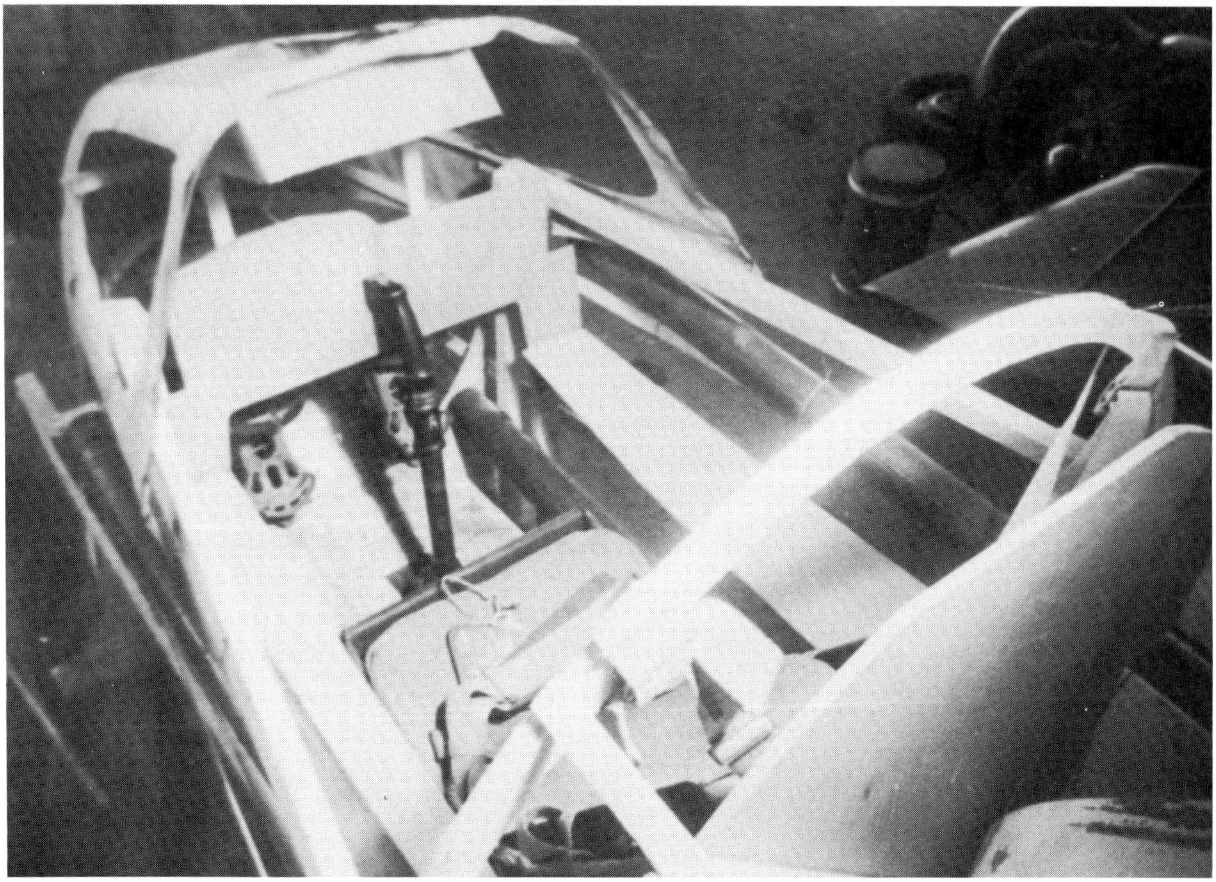

▲117 ▼118

117, 118. Two views of the Messerschmitt P.1112 mock-up, which was under construction on 18 April 1945 at the *Oberbayrische Forschungsanstalt* at Oberammergau in Bavaria. The P.1112 was a single-engined, tailless aircraft with a smaller fuselage than the P.1111. The project was planned alongside the P.1101, which was originally a fighter prototype but was later redesignated a high-speed research aircraft. The P.1110 and 1111 were submissions in the last German fighter competition of the war, along with the Focke-Wulf Ta 183, the Heinkel P.1078C and the Blohm & Voss P.209. Two other projects were finalized during April 1945, the redesigned Me 262 HG II and III, which featured modified flying surfaces.

119, 120. The Focke-Wulf Ta 183 was approved in early 1945, and plans were made to produce the Ta 183 V1 and seven further pre-production aircraft, together with two static test airframes. Three Ta 183 production versions were proposed, Ta 183A-1, A-2 and A-3, the first series aircraft being expected to fly early in 1946. The aircraft was to be powered by one Heinkel-Hirth HeS 011 (109-011) and armed with two or four heavy cannon. The Focke-Wulf '*Kampfjäger*', with MK 103s, was a parallel project.

121. Other late-war projects featured PTL 021 powerplants or a mixture of piston and turbojet engines. One of these was the Focke-Wulf '*Flitzer*', a wooden mock-up of which was built at Bad Eilsen in northern Germany in autumn 1944 showing a modern, well-equipped cockpit with good visibility for the pilot. One model of the '*Flitzer*' showed an He S11 A-1 and a Walter rocket motor. None of these designs was ever realized.

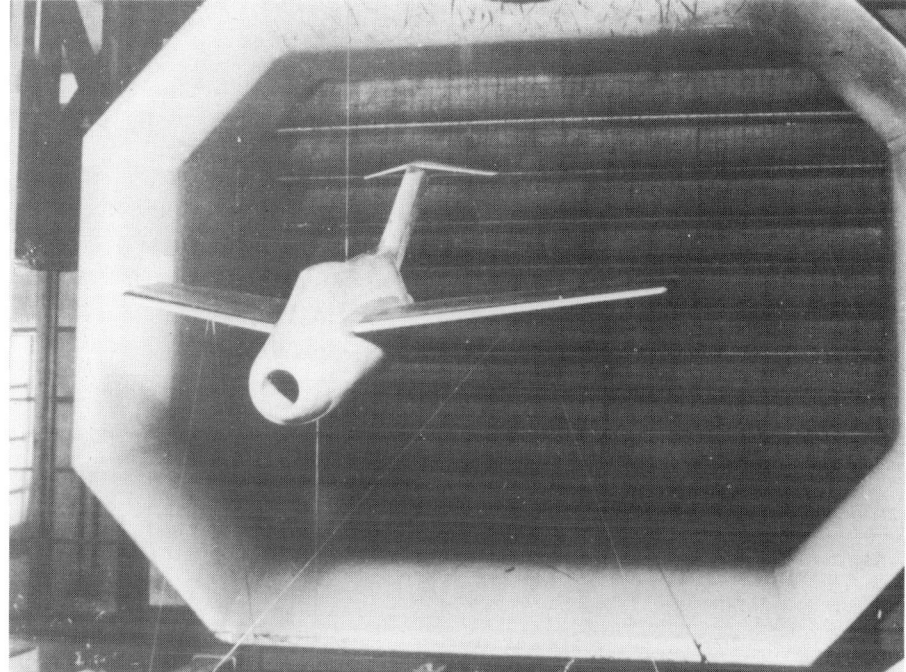

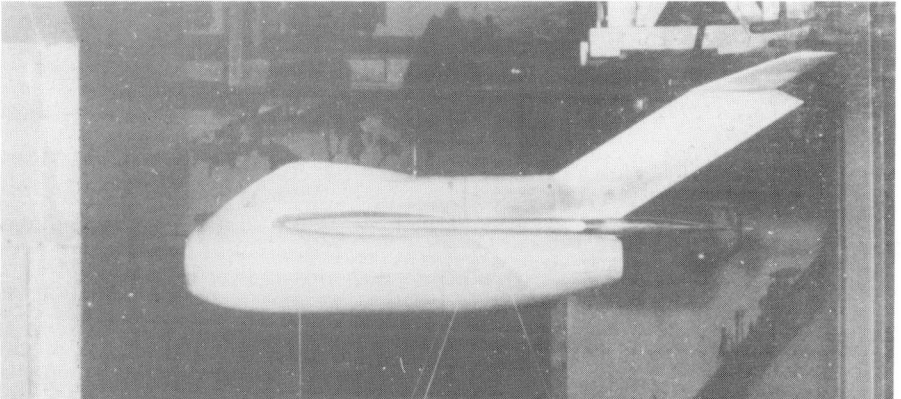

119 ▲

120 ▲   121 ▼

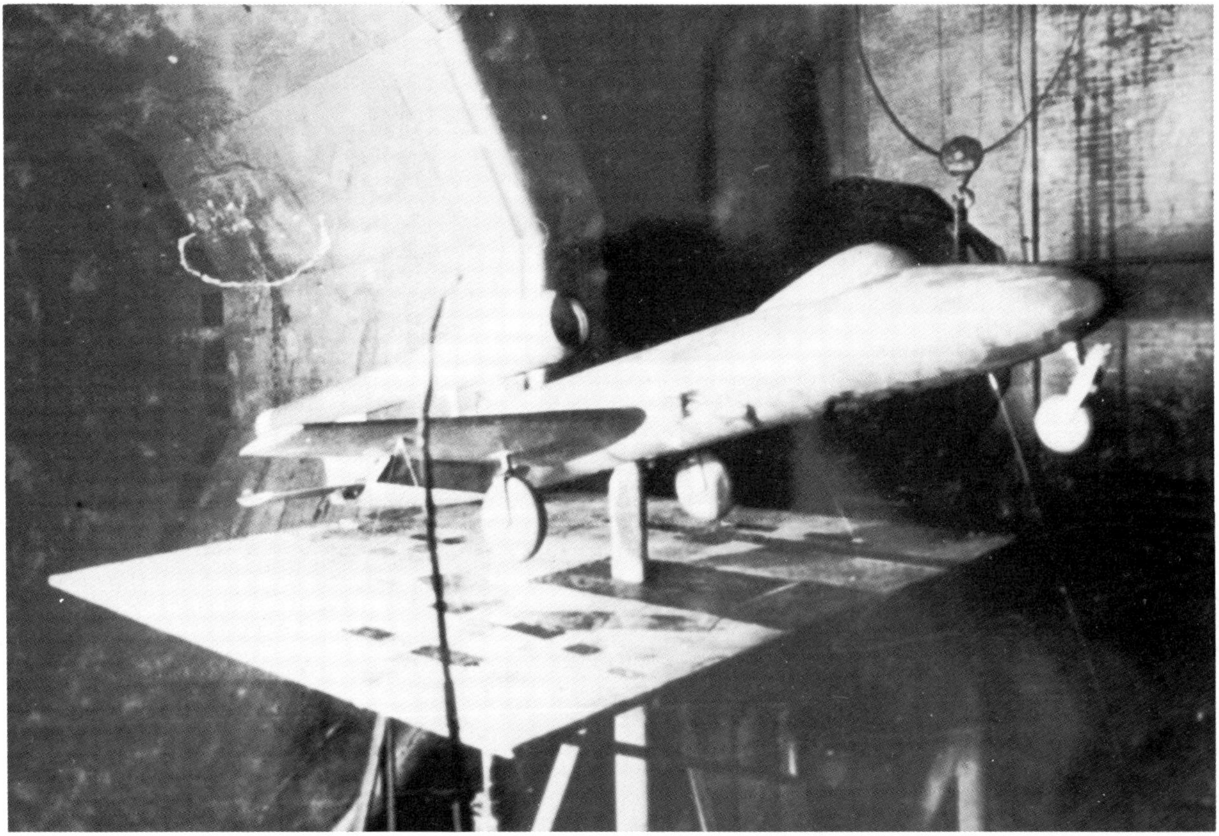

▲122   ▼123

124 ▲

122. Junkers made great efforts in the design of high-speed aircraft during 1944 and 1945. Projects known as *'Elly'* and *'Wally'*, the Junkers EF (*Entwicklungsflugzeug*, or experimental aircraft) 126 and 127, were tested as wind-tunnel models at Dessau, and development continued after May 1945 under Soviet management. There is a lot of evidence to suggest that serious attempts were made to get flight development underway: on 1 October 1945 Lt. Col. Olechnowitsch gave orders for a mock-up of the EF 126 to be built by October 20. The occupied Junkers factory was directed to manufacture five EF 126 aircraft, the first of which was to be rolled out on 1 February 1946 and the last on 20 April. However, all the German specialists were transferred to the Soviet Union before work was completed.

123. The DM 1, formerly known as the Lippisch P 13a, was a design for a high-speed fighter. Plans were finalized early in 1945, but about two months earlier, at the end of November 1944, a model of the P 13A with Lorin propulsion had flown for the fifteenth time over distances of more than 400ft, although the last flight resulted in the model's being severely damaged and the propulsion unit destroyed. The DM 1, which was Lippisch's first step towards creating a supersonic fighter

aircraft, was not completed until May 1945, and the sole example was captured at Prien airfield near Chiemsee in Bavaria and shipped to the United States.

124. The P 11 project was proposed towards the end of 1943 following a discussion between *Generalfeldmarschall* Milch and *Dipl-Ing*. Lippish about the latter's ideas for a high-speed bomber-destroyer. Some 240 personnel began work on the new aircraft, the first example of which was scheduled to be ready for unpowered flight in April or May 1944; the second P 11 would be equipped with two Jumo 004 jet engines, and two further aircraft, one for static tests, were also ordered. However, there was no production capacity for the advanced Lippisch studies.

125. One of the last German turbojet designs was the Me P.1101, a high-speed fighter aircraft developed at the top-secret *Oberammergau Forschungsanstalt* in the Bavarian Alps. It was planned to fit the first experimental aircraft with the Heinkel He S11A-1 turbojet, only a few of which were ever manufactured, at Zuffenhausen near Stuttgart. The He S11 was the most powerful turbojet engine built by German industry during the war, and a number of He S11A-0s were later produced under Allied management.

125 ▼

For an illustrated catalogue describing these and other books published by Arms & Armour Press, or if you wish to receive further information about specific subjects, please write to the address given on the back cover of this book, identifying your areas of interest.